THE FIVE
O'CLOCK
APRON

10 9 8 7 6 5 4 3 2 1

Ebury Press, an imprint of Ebury Publishing
20 Vauxhall Bridge Road
London, SW1V 2SA

Ebury Press is part of the Penguin Random
House group of companies whose addresses
can be found at:
global.penguinrandomhouse.com

Penguin
Random House
UK

Text © Claire Thomson 2015
Photography © Ebury Press 2015

Claire Thomson has asserted her right to
be identified as the author of this Work in
accordance with the Copyright, Designs
and Patents Act 1988

First published by Ebury Press in 2015

www.eburypublishing.co.uk

A CIP catalogue record for this book is
available from the British Library

Photography: Mike Lusmore
Illustrations: Alex Lucas
Editor: Annie Lee
Design: Interstate Creative Partners
Cover design: Two Associates

ISBN: 9780091958497

Colour origination by Altaimage
Printed and bound in China by
C & C Offset Printing Co., Ltd

Penguin Random House is committed to a
sustainable future for our business, our readers
and our planet. This book is made from Forest
Stewardship Council® certified paper

MIX
Paper from
responsible sources
FSC® C008047

For Grace, Ivy and Dorothy with love...
and plenty of vegetables.

CLAIRE THOMSON

THE FIVE O'CLOCK APRON

EBURY
PRESS

CONTENTS

I COOK, A LOT...

...often with the clock ticking and the 'I'm hungry' anthem gaining traction. Breakfast, lunch, supper. Snacks too. Children can eat an extraordinary amount, all things considered. It's therefore essential that this food is nutritious, delicious and relatively easy to produce. My background as a chef has helped enormously in this regard. When cooking for my three children (and often those of others), I try to cook with imagination, ease and, for the most part, speed. I am lucky. But for some, the task of producing food – day in, day out – seems like a relentless chore.

Short on time and week-night weary of imagination, it is all too easy to fall into a cookery loop. Spaghetti Bolognese Monday and shepherd's pie Thursday offer an easy, albeit lobotomizing, rhythm to the week. Children are notorious when it comes to what they will and won't put in their mouths. Contrary, wilful, at worst fussy, having to cajole kids into eating food they don't want is one of life's most frustrating, time-consuming and head-bangingly awful tasks.

Here's my suggestion: turn cooking on its head. Heal the schism in family cookery. The notion of children's food is something to baulk at. Smiley-faced food is ridiculous – food should look like food. Make food interesting. And children will then be interested in it. Children like flavour-FUL food, as do the grown-ups cooking and eating it themselves. Make vegetables core to the family diet. Make them exciting and joyful. Cook a cabbage with bulgur, tomato and garlic, 'sweeten' it with cinnamon and allspice and serve it with plain yoghurt to dollop and toasted seeds to sprinkle over. Where once cabbage might have sat untouched on the side of the plate, that same cabbage is now golloped greedily.

Having to cook separate food for children is laborious and unnecessary. Whether parents choose to eat an early supper with their children or whether it's eaten separately, the prospect of cooking just one meal is appealing. The recipes in this book are versatile enough to appease everyone and are transferable to a more adult-appropriate supper time (along with extra salt, perhaps, and a glass of wine).

More than just writing a book, in an apron and on a crusade, I'm keen to inspire and invigorate the concept of family cookery. Standing at the stovetop, I cook with affection and with an eye for sustenance.

Elbows down. Knives and forks at the ready, and we're off ...

HOW LONG IS A PIECE OF STRING?
HOW BIG IS A TEASPOON?
AND HOW MUCH IS A GLUG?

THOUGHTS ON MEASUREMENTS
AND OTHER KITCHEN TRAPPINGS...

SALT

When cooking for children, I am judicious with salt. If I do use salt, I tend to add it at the beginning of the cooking. This way what salt you do use will integrate better with the food and, so the theory goes, you then need less.

For food that is cooked with children in mind, then destined for grown-up consumption, I like to have some crunchy sea salt flakes or rock salt in a mill on the table to add per person, per plate. Salt is crucial to enhancing the flavour of food. I would far rather use salt wisely in my cooking at home and steer clear of more processed foods. That so many breakfast cereals and biscuits list salt as a key ingredient is something I find a mite malevolent.

With salt as such a matter of personal preference, I have found it tricky to be exacting about quantities in my recipes. Above all, food should be tasted throughout the cooking process. The term 'seasoning' (I use it often in this book) is a helpful reminder that food will always be specific to individual taste. Ingredients are seasoned with salt, pepper, spice or herbs according to who is eating them and with what they are being eaten.

OLIVE OIL

Again, in writing this book, I have found it agreeably problematic to nail exact measurements to the wall of my olive oil usage. A splush into a pan to sauté some vegetables might equate to a couple of tablespoons. A trickle on to some yoghurt to serve at the table with a pilaf might end up just being the one tablespoon. And while I am happy with the measurements given for olive oil in these recipes, they are guidelines. The adage 'how long is a piece of string' rings true for me, my cooking and that bottle of olive oil. Glug. Glug. Glug ...

That said, good olive oil is pricey and for this reason I never use the really good stuff to cook with. I much prefer to appreciate the flavour of good olive oil used to dress cooked food. A slick of fruity olive oil on top of some baked cannellini beans or lentils is magic. I cook with more ordinary everyday olive oils. A homemade tomato sauce wouldn't taste the same if not for the onion and garlic gently sweated in olive oil. It is worth noting, however, that olive oil does have a lower smoke point than vegetable or sunflower oil, so there really is little point in using olive oil when cooking anything that requires hard frying, as the oil can burn and become acrid.

BUTTER

The secret weapon of any chef, butter will make things taste unimaginably delicious and look both glossy and wonderful. I have previously worked in restaurants that make their mashed potato, almost but not quite, with more butter than potato. In home cooking, butter consumption is never quite as flagrant, of course. By all means use melted butter in lieu of oil for cooking in these recipes if you like.

One final thing on butter: brown butter is heaven sent – toasty, caramel buttery liquid spiked with a squirt of lemon juice. On its own spooned over grilled fish or partnered with plain yoghurt to dress vegetables, rice or lentil dishes, brown butter will make your food sing and your mouth water.

HERBS

I use an awful lot of herbs. They add flavour, vibrancy and freshness to food. But they surely are funny things to quantify. Basil in summer is incalculably different in taste, smell and herby punch to the pathetic supermarket packet airfreighted from afar and bought mid-winter. Use herbs seasonally and generously and you'll get more bang for your buck.

Hard herbs like rosemary, thyme, sage, oregano or bay I would encourage you to add at the beginning of the cooking time. For these herbs to permeate a dish, the longer they cook the better. Soft, bright herbs such as basil, mint, dill or marjoram like a showy late entrance to food. As for dried herbs, I avoid them, with the exception of dried mint or good-quality oregano dried on its stalk. Both give different and admirable qualities to cooking from their fresh alternatives.

Roughly speaking, in these recipes, a small bunch totals 15g of picked herbs and a large bunch 25g. Thyme leaves and rosemary needles I give as a spoon measurement.

CHILLI FLAKES

I like Turkish Aleppo or Urfa chilli flakes. Aleppo gives a medium heat with a sweet note and Urfa a smokier earthy hit. I buy mine from my local Turkish grocer, but have also seen them in Asian stores and online. Used in conjunction with salt as a table seasoning, these chilli flakes are deliciously addictive. Look out for the packets that have a sticky red residue clinging to the cellophane, as this moistness is a good thing and denotes fresher flakes.

SUGAR

Like salt, sugar is a contentious ingredient. We should be cautious about how much we use. That said, I like the sense of fulfilment to be had in making various sweet treats at home. Children like making cakes, biscuits

and puddings, and I'd be hesitant to demonize sugar by forbidding it. I am happy for my children to eat sweet things but on the basis of an occasional and delicious treat, and not a mainstay.

STOCK

Restaurants use a lot of stock. Great big vats of it are moved around the hob and jostle for stove space. Quite apart from giving a terrific foundation to cooking, stock made from scratch is a thrifty and thoughtful cookery practice to embrace. Buy good-quality meat and make stock from the bones. I find chicken or ham to be the most useful form of stock in the food I cook. I love the moment when I root through the freezer and find a forgotten tub of stock to use as a flavoursome base for a soup or braise.

LEMONS

I have an involuntary lemon-picking reflex. I cannot help myself buying one or two when food shopping. Just in case I don't have one in the fruit bowl at home. (I should note that this is almost unheard of.) The great big, imperfectly shaped sunshine-yellow ones with gnarled and cratered skin are my favourites, and unwaxed, even better. Quite apart from looking lovely, lemons flatter much of the food I cook. Lemons give counterpoint, lifting a dish and adding characteristic freshness and punch. Juice, flesh and zest – I love a lemon, I do.

SEASONED YOGHURT

By seasoned yoghurt I mean plain yoghurt with salt stirred in. Other additions – a scant clove of crushed garlic, lemon juice, a slick of olive oil, chilli flakes, fresh herbs, dried mint, grated raw vegetables (for raita/tzatziki) or ground sumac – are terrific too. Yoghurt served like this is a regular on the table, especially served alongside certain rice, spiced or vegetable dishes.

ROASTING SPICES

Absolutely and definitely worth doing. Have your pestle and mortar or spice grinder stationed beside the stovetop and leave it there to grind whole toasted spices for use in your cooking as and when. Into a dry frying pan go the whole spices, then snap, crackle, pop and at first whiff of the spicy smoke, they're ready to grind for a flavour that really resonates. Roasting spices and freshly grinding them does justice to their inclusion in a recipe.

TOMATO SAUCE

I always find it's worth making quite a big batch of tomato sauce, at least twice the quantity, refrigerating or freezing what I then don't use. A spoonful of well-made tomato sauce is both easy and a brilliant flavour supplement. Its versatility is endless. I am a fan of good-quality whole

tinned tomatoes and would always prefer to use these over an imported and out-of-season tomato. More of which later...

To skin fresh tomatoes, cut a small cross at the base of each one, place in bowl and pour over boiling water. After 1 minute, remove from the water and the skin should peel off easily.

MEAT THERMOMETER

I just can't imagine why anyone wouldn't have one of these at home. In a restaurant kitchen there is a certain amount of professionalism and kudos in knowing when a piece of meat or fish is perfectly cooked. Having to cook nine different rib-eye steaks on a grill and four orders of fish all in different pans, all of which started at different times, demands that chefs be in touch physically with the food they cook. A quick jab of a forefinger on the surface of a steak, or a deft lift of flesh from the bone on a tranche of fish to assess how well cooked it is, is a vital skill.

It isn't like this at home. A digital meat thermometer can tell you exactly whether something is perfectly done. It will assuage any fears about whether that enormous hunk of protein you have in the oven is cooked sufficiently. By all means gauge your cooking times just by touch, but a meat thermometer is an accurate and helpful tool. Use one in halloumi and yoghurt making and correct temperatures are no longer guesswork. Thermometers are cheap. Buy one.

WEIGHING

We have a beautiful old bright grass-green set of scales at home. Lugged back from Thailand (heavy and ridiculous in a back pack), it looks very lovely on the kitchen window ledge. It lives there unused. Less romantic, and given a good thrashing, are my digital scales. Measuring ingredients with the other set involved many little bowls each totalled up and tipped into a final mixing bowl.

It's a wonder to use a digital set, pressing zero each time I weigh a new addition, with each ingredient exact and housed in that same and final mixing bowl. I can weigh and mix a cake or some bread dough in minutes. For example, when making bread: ZERO 300g white flour ZERO 200g wholemeal flour ZERO 4g dried yeast ZERO 5g salt (and I even weigh the...) ZERO 375ml water.

Weighing liquids can take a bit of getting used to. Professional bakers will swear by it as a more precise method. Low-density liquids such as water or milk are easy to measure like for like in grams and will give by far the most accurate reading.

IN SHORT...

All eggs used here are free range and medium unless specified otherwise. Oil for dressings is extra-virgin olive, otherwise ordinary olive oil for cooking. All milk and yoghurt is full fat. All herbs are fresh. All parsley is flatleaf. All onions and garlic are peeled. All oven temperatures are fan... You get the general idea.

SERVES 4

Lastly, serves 4. Recipes given in this book are for the most part skewed to feed 4. But a world without leftovers would be a sorry one indeed. Roast a whole chicken with rice and spices and serve with yoghurt – by all means polish off the rice, but don't feel compelled to eat all the chicken. Serves 4, with some left over for the next day and a stock from the bones perhaps. Likewise, a tiny cake or too few muffins will never seem right.

Children, like adults, can also have very different sizes of appetite. 'Serves 4' is a guideline. 2 adults + 2 children. Or 3 adults. Or 2 hungry adults with leftovers. Or 6 children home for tea after school, one of whom is a baby. And so on. Phew.

MILK

The milky breath of a baby, a milky moustache frosted just so and the dulcet 'glug-glug-glug' of the milk bottle every morning. It's little wonder I begin with milk. A miracle drink and a marvellous ingredients to boot – we get through vast quantities of it in our house.

Not so long ago, we lived and worked near a dairy farm at the very tip of Cornwall. Rain, wind or shine (Christmas Day included), a heaving monochrome herd of cows would twice a day amble past our window en route to the milking sheds. Some days, I'd sit with Grace on the low stone wall and we'd watch these bovine beauties, heavy with milk, push and jostle each other along. Their walk back was lighter; it seemed to take them less time to reach the field. The spectacle left a road patchworked with poo, much to the amusement of my daughter and of those held up in their cars on those weaving Cornish lanes.

Occasionally we went with the farmer and collected milk to drink straight from the tap of the tank filled from the just-milked cows. Unpasteurized, warm, creamy rich and almost sweet, it was milk as I'd never tasted it before. From the restaurant kitchen, we could see the tanker arrive at dusk to collect that day's supply. With easy access to such a quantity of milk, any kitchen prep requiring lots of it also included a lovely five-minute yomp across the field to collect it.

There are innumerable recipes that use milk and here I give you my favourites. A basic béchamel sauce will set you up for very many meals. The alchemy of milk made rich and viscous with butter and flour and flavoured with nutmeg and bay leaf is masterful and has many uses. Making your own cheese and yoghurt is a captivating activity for children, and the results knock the socks off the shop-bought stuff.

BÉCHAMEL SAUCE (WHITE SAUCE)

A béchamel sauce is one of the first ever things I learnt to make on my own in the kitchen. Countless saucepans piled high, testament to multiple lumps and steely determination.

Making a good white sauce is essential and so versatile – it flatters many ingredients and children love the creamy unctuousness of it. Use it in pasta dishes, croque-monsieur and more besides.

~ ~ ~ ~

Makes about 600ml
- 600ml milk
- a few slices of onion
- 1 bay leaf
- ½ tsp black peppercorns
- 35g butter, plus extra for dotting on top if needed
- 35g plain flour
- salt and freshly ground black pepper
- freshly grated nutmeg (optional)

1. Bring the milk to the boil in a pan with the onion, bay leaf and peppercorns, then simmer for 2–3 minutes. Remove from the heat and allow to infuse for 10 minutes.

2. Meanwhile, in another pan, melt the butter, add the flour, stir to combine and cook over a low heat for a couple of minutes, stirring occasionally (the resulting paste is called a roux in restaurant kitchens).

3. Strain out the flavourings from the milk. Make sure that both the milk and roux are hot, then start gradually adding the milk to the roux, using a whisk. Whisk vigorously to make sure that no lumps form. (If you do get lumps, not to worry – they will often whisk out, or you can just strain the sauce through a fine sieve, pushing all the bits through, and begin whisking again in a new pan).

4. Cook the sauce very slowly for 15–20 minutes, stirring gently until it has thickened and is velvety.

5. Season with salt and pepper to your taste. Some recipes using béchamel are good with a little pinch of freshly grated nutmeg.

6. If not using straight away, dot the top of the sauce with butter or cover with a piece of baking parchment to stop a skin forming.

VARIATION: CHEESE SAUCE

If using the béchamel for a cheese sauce, add a handful of grated cheese (Cheddar, Gruyère) at the end of the cooking time – you only want the cheese to melt in the sauce, not cook in it.

YOGHURT

Yoghurt. We get through masses of it. There is the blob mixed with some stewed fruit to top a bowlful of Bircher muesli (see page 73) or porridge at breakfast. The dollop alongside buttery cinnamon or honey-spread toast. There's also the yoghurt blitzed into a lassi with water and some soft fruit that seems destined for the blender. Fast forward to lunch and supper, and it's a condiment – plain yoghurt is seasoned with a pinch of salt, chopped soft fresh herbs (dill, mint or coriander), a scraping of raw garlic and thinned with lemon juice to spoon over soups, dress vegetables or serve with a dhal.

Making your own yoghurt is easy. The initial pot will make four or five batches (any more and the flavour becomes almost too strong, and the setting ability of your yoghurt will decrease). Once in the rhythm of yoghurt-making, you'll be spurred on to use more in your cooking. Supply and demand: soon enough, yoghurt will be on everything.

~ ~ ~ ~

Makes about 750g
- 1 litre full-fat milk
- 100g live plain yoghurt (the ingredients information on the yoghurt container will confirm whether it contains live cultures)

1. Fill a large heavy pan not more than one-third full with the milk (so that it doesn't foam over the top of the pan). Bring to the boil over a moderate heat, stirring to prevent the milk sticking and burning, which would spoil the yoghurt.

2. Turn down the heat to a simmer (though do note that I often change pans at this point, as there can be milk stuck to the bottom of the pan that may burn) and reduce the liquid by about a quarter.

3. Remove the pan from the heat and pour the milk into a ceramic, glass or stainless-steel container to cool, which takes a good half hour or more. You want the milk not quite hot to the touch, about 32–36°C (if it is too hot it may kill the bacteria).

4. When the milk reaches this temperature, stir in the live yoghurt. Cover with a plate, a lid or clingfilm and put somewhere warm and draught-free. A turned-off oven with a pilot light, a thermos or an airing cupboard are all ideal, but if you have to leave the pan on the worktop it is best to wrap it in cloths to insulate it. If the room is too cool, the yoghurt will just take longer to incubate. The milk should not be disturbed while it turns into yoghurt.

5. The yoghurt is done when it has the consistency of custard, and it could be ready in about 4–6 hours, but I usually leave mine for about 8 hours because I do it overnight.

6. If you want to strain the yoghurt to thicken it, line a sieve with either cheesecloth, muslin, a handkerchief or a cotton cloth. Set it over a big bowl and pour the yoghurt into the cloth. Drain until it has achieved a consistency you like.

LEEK & YOGHURT SOUP

A Turkish method of soup-making that uses yoghurt as the base. To stop the yoghurt splitting (curdling), egg and cornflour are used to stabilize the ingredients. Magic – warm yoghurt, brown butter and toasted spices, with sweet earthy leeks and the aniseed notes of fresh dill.

~ ~ ~ ~

Serves 4
- 60g butter
- juice of ½ a lemon
- 50g sunflower seeds, toasted (see page 64)
- 4 medium leeks, sliced and very well washed
- salt and freshly ground black pepper
- 1 scant tbsp cornflour
- 2 egg yolks
- 500g plain yoghurt (see page 18)
- 2 cloves of garlic, crushed
- 1 tsp each cumin and coriander seeds, toasted and ground
- chilli flakes, to taste (optional)
- 450ml boiling water or chicken stock (see page 145), to thin the soup
- 1 small bunch of fresh dill, chopped

1. Put half the butter into a pan and cook over a moderate heat, stirring and scraping occasionally, until it foams and the sediment begins to turn golden brown, then add the lemon juice to stop the butter cooking any more. Pour the butter into a bowl, add the toasted sunflower seeds and keep somewhere warm.

2. Add the rest of the butter to the still hot pan and heat till it foams.

3. Add the leeks, season with a little salt and cook over a moderate heat till soft and sweet – about 20 minutes.

4. Meanwhile, in a bowl, beat the cornflour into the egg yolks, followed by the yoghurt, and set aside.

5. Add the garlic and ground spices to the leeks with a pinch of chilli flakes (if using) and cook for a couple of minutes more.

6. Turn down the heat to low and pour in the yoghurt mix, stirring well. Cook gently for a few minutes without letting it bubble/ simmer, as the soup will split if it gets too hot.

7. Add as much boiling water or stock as you need to thin the soup to your preference. I like to serve it fairly thick – almost porridge-like in consistency. Check the seasoning and add salt and pepper as needed.

8. Pour into bowls and top with the chopped dill, the reserved brown butter and more chilli flakes to taste.

LABNEH

Sweet or savoury, labneh is a doddle to make. My children like helping to roll this very thick strained yoghurt into little balls each the size of a walnut, to serve either steeped in olive oil and garlic to smear on flatbreads (see page 32), or drenched in icing sugar to serve with soft fruit as a pudding.

~ ~ ~ ~

Makes about 12 walnut-size balls
- ½ tsp salt
- 500g plain yoghurt (see page 18; if not homemade, use a thick Greek yoghurt)

1. Place a sieve over a bowl and line it with a double layer of clean cheesecloth or soft cotton fabric.

2. Stir the salt into the yoghurt, then pour the yoghurt into the centre of the cheesecloth. Pull up the four corners of the cheesecloth and tie them with string to make a bag, then suspend the bag over the bowl overnight to allow the whey to drain out. If your kitchen is cold enough, you can drain the yoghurt outside the fridge; otherwise leave it in the fridge. The longer you leave the labneh, the firmer it will become – after 12 hours it should be the consistency of cream cheese.

3. Remove from the cheesecloth and store the labneh, covered, in the fridge until needed.

4. To make the labneh balls, first ensure the labneh is firm enough to use a small spoon to scoop out little walnut-sized balls. Roll them between your hands to shape them, then place the balls on a clean cloth-lined tray to soak up any excess moisture.

5. Once the balls are made, I like to marinate them in a little olive oil (4 tablespoons for this quantity), some dried oregano or fresh thyme leaves (about 1 tablespoon), the zest of 1 lemon, and a few chilli flakes (¼ teaspoon). Store in the fridge.

VARIATION: SWEET LABNEH

Follow the recipe above, omitting the salt, and mix 50g of icing sugar into the yoghurt before straining. Serve with poached fruits (plums or rhubarb are nice), or with a spoonful of honey and alongside some oat cakes (see page 222). Better still, add 3 tablespoons of rose water with the icing sugar and serve the sweet rose labneh with strawberries or raspberries in the summer.

HALLOUMI CHEESE

Making cheese with children strikes a brilliant balance between a kind of whiz-bang chemistry and gentle alchemy. It is a mesmerizing sight for kids when such a quantity of milk solidifies with just a few teaspoons of rennet. I use a vegetarian rennet, which has always given consistent results. It also saves you an explanation on the somewhat squeamish origins of animal rennet.

This recipe requires quite a lot of milk. From this you will get the cheese and also the whey. This surplus liquid can be salted and used as a brine should you want to store your cheese for longer than three or four days (doing so will make it more like the salty, squeaky shop-bought halloumi). Or you can use the whey in any bread-making recipes that require water. The watery whey will enhance the flavour of the dough.

~ ~ ~ ~

Makes 800g
- 5 litres full-fat milk
- 25ml Langdale's vegetarian essence of rennet (available from all good health food shops) or other vegetarian rennet (in which case check the packet instructions for amount)
- salt

1. Gradually bring the milk up to 32–36°C (blood temperature) in a wide-bottomed pan (I use a meat thermometer, but you could use any type of thermometer as long as it will record a temperature up to 85°C).

2. Add the rennet, stirring gently. Let the mixture settle for 1 hour. It will set like a junket or jelly.

3. Cut the curd into roughly 2cm cubes – do this by slicing the mixture with a long thin-bladed knife. The curd will come away from the watery whey – leave it to settle for half an hour.

4. Bring the curds and whey mixture up to about 38°C on a very gentle heat over a period of about 30 minutes.

5. Using a slotted spoon, scoop the curds into, ideally, a perforated container lined with muslin or a fine tea towel (though a sieve would do equally well) with another container beneath it to collect the extra whey.

6. If the draining curds are thicker than a few centimetres, it might be a good idea to weight them down with a plate or other suitable object. Leave to drain until firm, about 1 hour.

7. When you are ready to poach the curds, heat the whey to 85°C and add 1 tablespoon of salt.

8. When you are ready to cut the curd, turn the cheese out on to a board and slice into oblongs about 5cm wide.

9. Ensure your whey is at 85°C and gently place the cheese blocks in the hot whey. When the cheese rises to the top of the liquid, it is ready. Place back into your cleaned draining container. The cheese will be quite fragile at first but will firm up quickly as it cools. (Retain the whey if brining the cheese – see next step.)

10. Once cooled, you can either serve the cheese pan-fried fresh (as we like to), or you may wish to brine it, as it will then keep for a month or so in the fridge (500ml of the whey to 500ml of boiling water with 100g salt – pour the cooled salty liquid over the cheese and keep immersed in an airtight container) – this will give a taste and texture more similar to commercially produced halloumi.

EASY PEASY
ROSE ICE CREAM

Used as an ingredient, rose water offers sweetly perfumed rosy notes that are particularly flattering in creamy puddings. In this ice cream, similar to an Indian kulfi, the rose water goes especially well with the dusky sweetness of the evaporated milk.

~ ~ ~ ~

Makes about 500g

- 1 x 410ml tin of evaporated milk
- 130g caster sugar
- 60ml rose water (see note below)

1. Refrigerate the tin of evaporated milk the night before you plan on making your ice cream.
2. In a bowl, using an electric whisk, whip the cold evaporated milk with the sugar until doubled in size and ribbons from the beaters trailing through the mix begin to form – this should take a good 10 minutes.
3. Add the rose water and beat for a few seconds.
4. Pour the mix into an ice-cream maker and churn as per the machine's instructions, or simply pour the whipped mix into a tub, lid it and freeze immediately.
5. Freeze for at least a couple of hours before eating. If eating the ice cream several days after making it, you may need to remove it from the freezer 30 minutes before serving to make it easier to scoop.

VARIATION

By all means play around with flavours – use vanilla extract instead of rose water, throw in some raspberries as you churn the mix, or add some maple syrup and a handful of walnuts. Experiment: this method is fairly foolproof.

BUTTERMILK
& RHUBARB PUDDINGS

Beats a jelly any day. The perfect milky wobble with soft fruit beneath. A riff on those supermarket fruit-layer yoghurts, if you like – use any soft fruit. I just like the rosy tones of the pink rhubarb with the white of the buttermilk.

~ ~ ~ ~

Makes 4 large or 6 small puddings, set in glasses

For the rhubarb
- 2 large sticks of rhubarb, trimmed and cut into 5cm lengths
- 40g caster sugar

For the buttermilk
- 1 leaf of gelatine
- 100ml milk
- 40g caster sugar
- ½ a vanilla pod, or vanilla extract to taste
- 300ml buttermilk (or yoghurt thinned with milk)
- 100ml double cream

1. Preheat the oven to 200°C/gas mark 6 and place 4 large or 6 small serving glasses in the fridge to chill.

2. Put the rhubarb into an ovenproof dish, scatter over the sugar and add a splash of water. Cover the dish with foil and bake for 15 minutes, or until the rhubarb is soft. Remove from the oven and leave to cool.

3. Strain the rhubarb well and distribute between the chilled glasses. The leftover juice can be mixed with fizzy water to make a lovely drink (see page 237).

4. Soak the gelatine in a bowl of cold water for 5 minutes, until soft.

5. In a small pan, bring the milk, sugar and vanilla pod or extract to the boil, then remove from the heat.

6. Drain the gelatine, squeeze dry, add to the warm milk and whisk to melt the gelatine. Let the milk mixture cool down to room temperature, then remove the vanilla pod, if using (scraping any seeds into the milk), and mix the buttermilk into the cooled milk.

7. Whip the cream to soft peaks, then stir or whisk the buttermilk mixture into the cream. Gently pour on top of the rhubarb in the glasses, and chill for at least 2 hours before serving.

BREAD

More than just the sides of a sandwich, bread is a cornerstone of family eating. The sheer versatility of bread as an ingredient marks it, for me, as one of the most important.

Making bread and using bread in cookery are very different things. To make bread is to bake. To use bread with innovation is to cook well. Both are practices I find utterly compelling.

I have worked as a baker in a restaurant (albeit on the Monday slot – quieter and not with the hair-raising demands of a weekend's bread needs). Once a week, and well before sunrise, I was the first to interrupt the thrum of the fridges, snap on the lights and fire up the ovens. Those baking shifts were very different from the machismo and cacophony of my usual cheffing stints.

The hush and solitude, the sense of growth and life as the doughs expand ... Night turns to day. The bulk of the work all but finished as a caffeine-craving flock of chefs descends on the kitchen.

Baking with children is a different proposition. While certainly not peaceful, what strikes me about baking bread with kids is the fun that the journey from flour to dough to loaf presents. I have baked with many children of various ages and aptitudes, and find it universal in its appeal.

For a child, flour isn't simply something you cook with. It's rain, it's snow, it's magic puffing powder. It's a funny moustache and ghoulish face dust. It changes the colour of your clothes and hair and can be sprinkled on the floor to make a path to skip through. It is so much more than just an ingredient.

Once in a bowl with water, yeast, salt and perhaps olive oil and given a good kneading, the pillowy mass begins to grow and grow. Children are always amazed by this sense of 'aliveness', and the moment of truth is when you shape the dough into loaves for baking. Carefully tucked into tins for one more rest before baking, these plump dough babies begin to seem more nurtured, more alive, than ever. Children always care about the bread they bake.

With bread as an ingredient, its cookability is determined by its age. And if I'm honest (for I'm a cook, not a baker, after all), I relish the possibilities that a couple-of-days-old sourdough loaf presents. It goes without saying that the snowy-white sliced stuff laced with preservatives will never age gracefully and the only loaf worth cooking with is a well-made one.

BASIC
BREAD DOUGH

Hand on heart, this is very, very easy. With almost no kneading, the dough is wetter than you might expect, and as a result I find this method infallible. We have a brilliant bakery nearby, and if it's a sourdough loaf or Saturday pastries I'm after, I know where to go. But for sandwiches and daily bread, I'll often make my own.

Of a morning, when I'm making tea, buttering toast, brushing children's teeth, tumbling things into a lunchbox, hunting for socks, hairbands, book bags and firing out spellings, I'll still find the time to hurl a measuring bowl on to the scales, tip in some flour, yeast, salt and measure in the water – a speedy stir with a spoon until formed and cover with a damp tea towel. Five minutes. Tops.

Busy, forgetful or simply my day running away with me, there the bowl might sit for one, two, maybe three hours, on occasion even as long as home from school, when I'll tip the dough out, give it a good knead on an oiled surface and pop it into a tin. Where it'll sit and wait for another hour or so before being baked into a loaf or other item.

This recipe makes:
- 1 tin loaf (see right)
- 10 flatbreads (see page 32)
- 12 snail bread (see page 248)
- 30 or so breadsticks (see page 217)
- 1 focaccia (see page 230)
- about 8 lahmacun (see page 159)

- 300g strong white bread flour (use 500g if you want a 100 percent white loaf), plus extra for sprinkling
- 200g strong wholemeal flour
- 5g salt
- 1 level tsp (4g) dried yeast
- 375g cold water
- about 2 tbsp olive oil, for oiling your hands, work surface and loaf tin

1. Put the flour, salt and yeast into a big mixing bowl.

2. Add the water. Cold water is fine to use. The prove doesn't need to be jump-started by warm water. A slower prove makes for better bread.

3. Using a large metal spoon, give the ingredients a vigorous mixing to combine. After a minute or so of mixing, the dough should be cohesive and pulling away from the sides of the bowl in a big ball. It will feel wet. It should do: don't be tempted to add more flour.

4. Cover the bowl with a clean, damp tea towel and leave to rest on the worktop for an hour or more – you want the dough to approximately double in size.

5. Turn the dough out on to a lightly oiled work surface and knock it back with lightly oiled hands, pushing, folding and turning the dough back in on itself for a good few minutes.

6. If making a loaf of bread, shape into a loaf shape – tucking and folding the seams to sit on the underside. Lightly oil a 450g loaf tin, put the loaf into the tin with the damp tea towel over the top and rest for a further 30–45 minutes.

7. After resting, each piece of dough should have not quite doubled in size again – just rising above the lip of the tin is sufficient. You want the dough to still have a bit of unexpended energy from the yeast, so that when it hits the heat of the very hot oven, the loaves will give a final burst upwards.

8. Preheat the oven to 220°C/gas mark 7.

9. Using a sharp serrated bread knife, gently make a cut about 1cm deep along the surface of the loaf. Sprinkle a pinch or two of extra flour over the top of the loaf.

10. Cook the loaf for 10 minutes, then turn the oven temperature down to 190°C/gas mark 5. Continue to cook for 25–30 minutes.

11. To test if the loaf is ready, tip it out of the tin and give it a good tap from beneath. It should sound hollow and the loaf should have a good crust.

12. Rest on a wire rack for at least 45 minutes before cutting (preferably for an hour or so).

FLATBREADS

Makes 5 flatbreads

- ½ recipe of basic bread dough (see page 30), made up to step 5 of the method
- extra strong white flour, for dusting and rolling
- 1 tbsp olive oil, plus extra for oiling the baking sheet
- 1 tbsp mixed whole small seeds (sesame, nigella, cumin, coriander, etc.)

1. Preheat the oven to 230°C/gas mark 8.
2. Divide the dough into 5 balls.
3. On a well-floured surface, use a rolling pin to gently roll out and stretch each dough ball into an oval or whatever shape is easiest for you. You want to get the dough about 4mm thick.
4. Place the flatbreads on an oiled baking sheet (or a hot pizza stone) and lightly oil the tops, then sprinkle with whatever seeds you are using.
5. Bake on the top shelf of the oven for 5–8 minutes, until bubbled up and coloured, but not completely crisp.

VARIATION: PIZZA

You can use the flatbread recipe above to make 2 pizzas. Use the tomato sauce recipe on page 172. I find it best to sprinkle a handful of diced mozzarella over the pizza base halfway through the cooking, so that the cheese doesn't overcook in the time it takes for the base to become perfectly crisp. Dress while hot with a slug of olive oil and lots of fresh basil for a Margherita-style pizza.

CROQUE-MONSIEUR

The 'croque' refers to the crunch of this fried cheese and ham sandwich. This Mr is made all the mightier by the addition of leftover béchamel sauce smeared generously between the slices. A croque-madame is a monsieur with a hole stamped out into which you crack an egg and fry it at the same time as the sandwich. Truly a mighty Mrs.

~ ~ ~ ~

Makes 4

- 20g softened butter, plus another 30g for cooking
- 8 slices of good-quality bread
- 200g well-flavoured leftover béchamel (see page 16)
- 200g Gruyère, Emmental or a good Cheddar cheese
- 4 thick slices of good ham
- 2 tbsp Dijon mustard
- 4 eggs (if making a madame – see below)

1. Butter one side of each slice of bread and set aside.
2. Divide the slices into pairs. Spread the cold béchamel on one slice, grate the cheese over and put a slice of ham on top. Spread the Dijon mustard on the other slice and sandwich the two slices firmly together. Repeat with the rest of the bread.
3. Heat a large frying pan over a medium-high heat until moderately hot and add a knob of butter.
4. Add as many sandwiches as will fit into the pan and fry, turning once, until they are golden brown and crisp. Repeat with the remaining sandwiches, adding more butter to the pan if necessary.
5. Drain on kitchen paper, cut into pieces and serve straight away, wrapped in paper napkins or greaseproof paper.
6. Alternatively, the sandwiches can be cooked under the grill until browned on each side. Try not to have the grill too hot, so that the filling has time to melt before browning.

VARIATION: CROQUE-MADAME

Follow the instructions for a monsieur, above, then use a pastry cutter to cut a hole in the centre of the sandwich. Preheat the oven to 200°C/gas mark 6, then, using an ovenproof frying pan that will fit your oven, fry one side of the croque until nicely coloured. Turn it over and crack an egg into the hole, then put the pan into the oven to continue cooking for about 4–6 minutes, or until the egg white is set.

SUMMERY FATTOUSH

Best to make this chopped bread salad when ingredients are in season and full of flavour, so here I offer you both a summery and a wintry fattoush (see page 36). Sumac gives the salad its characteristic tang. Try to chop the vegetables roughly uniform in size, so that each mouthful has an equal mix of this and that.

~ ~ ~ ~

Serves 4

- 4 pitta breads or flatbreads
- 75ml olive oil
- 500g ripe tomatoes or cherry tomatoes, chopped
- 1 bunch of spring onions, sliced
- 150g radishes, finely sliced
- 1 cucumber, peeled, deseeded and chopped
- 2 baby gem lettuces, or other crunchy lettuce, chopped
- 1 large bunch of fresh flat-leaf parsley, roughly chopped
- 1 small bunch of fresh mint, roughly chopped
- 1 large lemon (preferably unwaxed)
- 1 clove of garlic, crushed
- salt and freshly ground black pepper
- 2 tsp sumac
- 1 tsp chilli flakes (optional)

1. Preheat the oven to 180°C/gas mark 4.
2. Cut the pitta bread into approximately 2.5cm squares, place on a baking tray and toss with 3 tablespoons of the olive oil. Bake in the oven for 10 minutes, until toasted and golden. Put to one side.
3. Put all the chopped salad vegetables into a large bowl with the toasted pitta and add the chopped herbs.
4. To make the dressing, juice the lemon, finely grate the zest, and put into a bowl with the rest of the olive oil. Add the crushed garlic, to taste. Pour the dressing over the assembled salad and mix well, adding salt and pepper to taste.
5. Sprinkle the salad with the sumac and chilli flakes (if using).
6. You can serve the fattoush immediately or, if you'd rather, leave it for half an hour for the flavours to mingle and the pitta to absorb the dressing – giving you a chewier rather than crisp pitta.

VARIATIONS

Serve with 100g of feta crumbled through, or with some salted labneh balls (see page 20) on the side, or alongside some grilled or barbecued meat/fish or the brick chicken (see page 140).

WINTRY
FATTOUSH

Use the same method as on page 34, but replace the summer vegetables with this winter selection. Use all of these raw.

~ ~ ~ ~

Serves 4

- 4 pitta breads or flatbreads
  (see page 32)
- 3 tbsp olive oil
- 1 fennel bulb, trimmed
  and thinly sliced
- 1 medium carrot, peeled and sliced
  into thin rounds with a potato peeler
- ½ a medium cauliflower, trimmed of
  leaves and broken into tiny florets
- 1 parsnip, peeled and core removed,
  sliced thinly using a potato peeler
- 200g curly kale or cabbage, stalk
  removed, thinly sliced
- 1 small red onion, thinly sliced
- 1 small chicory or radicchio,
  thinly sliced
- seeds from 1 whole pomegranate
- 1 pear, peeled, cored
  and thinly sliced
- 50g walnuts, roughly chopped
- 1 small bunch of fresh dill,
  roughly chopped
- 1 small bunch of fresh flat-leaf
  parsley, roughly chopped
- 1 tsp sumac
- a pinch of chilli flakes (optional)

For the dressing

- juice of 1 small lemon
- 80ml olive oil
- 2 tbsp pomegranate molasses
- 1 small clove of garlic, crushed
- ¼ tsp ground cinnamon
- ½ tsp salt

1. Toss the pitta bread with the oil and toast as in the summery fattoush recipe.

2. Put all the vegetables, fruit, walnuts, herbs and spices into a bowl as for the summery fattoush (see page 34), then mix all the dressing ingredients together and pour over the assembled salad.

PANGRATTATO
(FRIED BREADCRUMBS)

I think I love pangrattato most because I've also seen it go by the name 'Poor Man's Parmesan' (in poorer parts of southern Italy, pangrattato was used as a substitute for expensive Parmesan cheese). Leftover bread is whizzed into breadcrumbs and baked with a rosemary-and-garlic-flavoured olive oil. Crisp toasted and roasted nuggets of bread to scatter over pasta or vegetables or in salads to give extra flavour and utterly addictive crunch. I have a jam jar of pangrattato on the go at all times. It is replenished whenever there is old bread that needs using up. With the additional sidekick of chilli flakes, this combination is a winner.

~ ~ ~ ~

Makes 1 large jar

- 60ml olive oil
- 2 cloves of garlic, unpeeled and slightly squashed
- 300g (about ⅓ of a loaf) good-quality bread, crusts removed and made into crumbs (not too fine – they can be crushed further after cooking if you want them smaller)
- 1 large sprig of fresh rosemary

1. Heat the olive oil in a thick-bottomed pan over a moderate heat and add the garlic. Continue to cook until the cloves turn golden.

2. Remove the garlic, then add the breadcrumbs and rosemary to the hot garlic-flavoured oil and stir well. Cook the breadcrumbs, stirring all the while, until they turn golden and crisp.

3. Using a slotted spoon, transfer the crumbs and rosemary to a plate lined with kitchen paper or a clean tea towel to absorb any excess oil.

4. Leave the oil to cool in the pan, then pour it through a sieve to use another time.

WHITE
SODA BREAD

No kneading. No proving. Bread that can be on the breakfast table in 45 minutes. Scone-like. Cloud-like. Make some. And then make the spotted version.

~ ~ ~ ~

Makes 2 loaves
- a handful of rolled oats
- 375g plain flour, plus extra for dusting
- 5g salt
- 8g bicarbonate of soda
- 300ml buttermilk (or yoghurt thinned with milk)

1. Preheat your oven to 200°C/gas mark 6 and sprinkle a baking sheet with a few oats – half a handful is plenty.

2. Sift the flour into a wide bowl with the salt and bicarbonate of soda.

3. Make a well in the centre of your flour mix and begin pouring the buttermilk in gradually, stirring gently with a wooden spoon. The trick of good soda bread is to not mix it too much, but to mix it enough so that the mixture forms a nice sticky cohesive mass in the centre of the bowl. You need to be confident to mix it enough to form a dough, but not too much for it to become stodgy and overworked.

4. When you have the dough right, lightly flour your work surface and tip your dough on to it. Separate the dough into 2 equal pieces and ever so gently pat them into a round-ish form. Slash the top of each as if it were a hot cross bun and place on a baking sheet lined with baking parchment. Sprinkle liberally with oats.

5. Bake in the middle of the oven for 35–45 minutes, checking after 20 minutes that the loaves aren't scorching. They should look tawny brown and wonderfully knobbly. Tap the underside of each loaf – it should sound hollow.

6. Cool on wire racks and eat just warm, with plenty of butter. After one day this bread is best eaten toasted.

VARIATION: SPOTTED SODA BREAD

Make as above – but reduce the salt to a good pinch, add 10g of caster sugar and 50g of currants to the flour and bicarbonate of soda and mix well before adding the buttermilk. Bake as before.

SAUSAGE & CAULIFLOWER BREAD PUDDING

Bread and butter pudding, but with sausages and cauliflower. Savoury bread puddings are a wonder. Omit the sausage and add mushrooms if you like.

~ ~ ~ ~

Serves 4

- 3 bay leaves
- 1 dsp fennel seeds
- 1 dsp picked fresh thyme leaves (keep the stalks)
- salt and freshly ground black pepper
- 1 small cauliflower, broken into florets
- 25g butter
- 25g plain flour
- 100ml pouring cream
- 1 dsp red wine vinegar
- 1 tsp Dijon mustard
- 4 fat sausages or 6 smaller ones (Toulouse are nice)
- 2 tbsp olive oil
- 3 cloves of garlic, finely sliced
- 350g crusty white bread, 2–3 days old, roughly sliced and each slice cut into 3
- ½ a radicchio, roughly sliced (optional)
- 60g Parmesan cheese, freshly grated

1. Preheat the oven to 180°C/gas mark 4.

2. Bring a large pan of water to the boil with the bay leaves, fennel seeds, reserved thyme stalks and a good pinch of salt – you need enough water to cover and cook the cauliflower, and for the final quantity of water to total at least 400ml.

3. Add the cauliflower to the water and cook until tender, about 5 minutes. Drain and reserve the herby cauliflower water to make the sauce – the fennel seeds are fine left in. Extract the thyme stalks and bay leaves. Set aside the cooked florets.

4. Return the pan to the heat. Over a moderate heat, melt the butter, add the flour, combine and stir for a couple of minutes (the resulting paste is called a roux).

5. Add 400ml of the hot herby cauliflower water gradually to the roux and whisk vigorously each time to ensure no lumps form before adding more. Turn down the heat and cook the sauce for about 10 minutes, stirring often, until the sauce has thickened and is the consistency of double cream.

6. Add the cream, vinegar and Dijon mustard and add salt and pepper to taste.

7. Meanwhile, squeeze out the meat from the sausages. Heat the oil in a large frying pan over a moderate heat. When hot, add the sausage meat and fry for 3 minutes, until roughly broken up and browning in places. Add the garlic and continue to cook for another 2 minutes. Add the pieces of bread and the thyme leaves and give it all a good stir over a low heat for another 2 minutes. Take off the heat, add the cooked cauliflower pieces and the radicchio (if using), and give it another thorough mix.

8. To assemble the pudding, spread the contents of the pan in a large (approx. 28 x 20cm) baking dish in one even layer. Pour the sauce over the top then sprinkle over the Parmesan.

9. Cook in the oven for 40–45 minutes, until bubbling and with some of the bread on the top going crisp and golden brown.

10. Serve with a great big green salad.

BREAD
SAUCE

The perfect accompaniment to roast birds, bread sauce triumphs at Christmas. To transform the sauce into an even sturdier side dish, pour it into a greased ovenproof dish and bake for 15 minutes at 180°C/gas mark 4. Serve warm, cut into firm wedges.

~ ~ ~ ~

Serves 4

- 1 small onion, halved
- 60g butter
- salt and freshly ground white pepper
- 8 cloves
- 1 large bay leaf
- 600ml full-fat milk
- a few scrapes of freshly grated nutmeg
- 110g fresh white breadcrumbs
- 2 tbsp double cream (optional)

1. Finely chop one half of the onion and cook gently in a pan with half the butter and a pinch of salt over a moderate heat until soft and translucent.
2. Stud the other onion half with the cloves, pushing them through the bay leaf to stick it on to the onion.
3. Put the milk and studded onion into the pan of cooked onion, then bring to the boil and simmer gently for 5 minutes.
4. Remove from the heat, add the nutmeg and leave the sauce to infuse for about an hour.
5. Remove the studded onion from the pan.
6. Stir the breadcrumbs into the milk and place the saucepan on a very low heat, stirring now and then, until the breadcrumbs have swollen and thickened the sauce – this should take about 15 minutes.
7. When thick, stir in the remaining 30g of butter and the cream (if using). Add salt and pepper to taste.
8. Pour into a warm serving jug.

VARIATION: BREAD SAUCE WITH MUSHROOMS

Add a handful of finely chopped soaked dried porcini (or other dried mushrooms) with the chopped sautéd onion at the beginning. Be sure to use some of the mushroom-soaking liquid in lieu of some of the milk – about a third should do – for a mushroom-rich bread sauce. This version is especially good with game birds.

BROWN BREAD ICE CREAM

This cheaty ice cream method is a marvel. Whip a cold can of evaporated milk until voluminous, then flavour and freeze. You can tip the mix into a container to freeze or, if you'd rather (and I would), use an ice-cream maker to churn and freeze the mix.

As for the brown bread, the crumbs are caramelized in a pan beforehand with butter and sugar, then added to the mix to yield praline-like nutty chewy bits. The cinnamon is optional, but I think it flatters the toasty notes of the brown bread.

~ ~ ~ ~

Makes 500g

- 50g butter
- 100g day-old brown bread, blitzed into breadcrumbs
- 80g demerara sugar
- 2 tsp ground cinnamon (optional)
- 1 x 410ml tin of evaporated milk, refrigerated overnight

1. In a wide pan, melt the butter over a moderate heat. Add the breadcrumbs and stir for 5 minutes, so that the crumbs toast and turn crunchy and golden.

2. Add half the sugar – the crumbs will clump to the sugar – and keep stirring for another 3 minutes until the sugar has all melted. Don't let the sugary breadcrumbs colour too much. Add the cinnamon (if using) and take off the heat. The breadcrumbs should be nicely caramelized and walnut brown.

3. Whip the cold evaporated milk in a bowl with the remaining sugar until doubled in size and the mix begins to form ribbons when the beaters are trailed through – this should take a good 10 minutes. Add the cooled crisp breadcrumbs and stir until well combined.

4. Churn in an ice-cream maker and freeze, or tip into a plastic container and immediately freeze.

5. Leave in the freezer for a couple of hours. Remove from the freezer 30 minutes before serving.

EGGS

It was when my daughter Grace, aged three at the time and standing in a chicken coop at a friend's house, stray feathers and kitchen compost all about her, asked me how chickens were chickens and eggs were eggs, that I clumsily conjured up an explanation – part chicken-and-egg fable, part misspent school biology classes.

The crux of the matter for Grace seemed to be how we knew whether an egg would house a chick or the gloopy stuff she knew as raw egg. With no cockerel in the coop, it's safe to imagine the destiny of these particular eggs was the waiting breakfast table. But the possibility that an egg could turn out be a chicken clearly confused her.

She was only three (the mating skills of cockerels could wait a wee while) and I've since read and re-read up on all things egg-related should I find myself on egg-collection duty with my other daughters any time soon.

It takes a hen about twenty-five hours to make an egg. The process is a compelling one. Kept for domestic egg consumption, a hen can lay an egg a day for a year or more. The miracle of the egg is the versatility of its vessel. Fertilized, an egg will house and feed the growing chick inside. In a nut(egg)shell: when rooster sperm meets hen egg cells outside the ovary and before the shell is formed in the oviduct – BINGO – egg becomes chicken. Unfertilized, these nutrients and proteins go on to become one of the cook's most trusted ingredients.

Sweet or savoury in application, eggs are genius. Breakfast, lunch, teatime and supper. Midnight snack. Elevenses. Picnics. Packed lunches and everything in between. Baked, boiled, fried, scrambled and pickled. Beaten, whipped, coddled and poached. Providing elevation and puff, gloss and varnish, silken smoothness, the power to clarify and also emulsify – egg as ingredient is astounding.

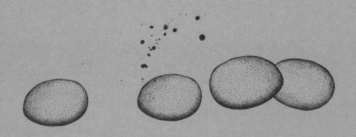

SPANISH TORTILLA

I had to make two or three tortillas every evening before service at the very first restaurant I ever worked in. The task was always charged with a sense of competitiveness from whichever chef one was working alongside that night. With time on our side and the prep list complete, sometimes (not often) there would be a tortilla-off, with two chefs each making a tortilla in their own exacting style. A blind taste test would then ensue, led by the ever-peckish waiting staff, and that evening's tortilla champ would then be crowned. I was the baby in that kitchen and it took a wee while for me to earn my tortilla stripes. More than ten, certainly less than thirty – TOO runny, TOO cooked, TOO burnt, TOO something; anyhow, this is my way and it's pretty much spot on. Thud goes the gauntlet as it hits the kitchen floor.

Tortilla purists would not use a spoon to make a tortilla, using only the pan to shake and move the mix around to form the crust, but I think spooning the mix a little before forming the crust gives greater control in the cooked vs runny egg ratio. Likewise frying the potatoes in oil to cook them from raw is best – in a restaurant kitchen this is easy, with a deep-fat fryer set low and a large basket to fry the potatoes in. Using boiled potatoes mixed in the oniony oil, I feel, is a fine interpretation when making tortillas at home.

Serves 4
- about 5 tbsp olive oil
- 2 medium Spanish onions, sliced
- salt and freshly ground black pepper
- 500g waxy potatoes, peeled, sliced into 1cm rounds and boiled until just tender (or you can use any left over from a previous meal)
- 5 eggs

1. Heat 4 tablespoons of the olive oil in a large heavy-bottomed saucepan and when hot add the onions and a pinch of salt. Reduce the heat to low and cook slowly, stirring every 3 minutes or so, for about 10–15 minutes, until golden and smelling sweet. Remove from the heat, drain, and reserve the oil.

2. Return the oil to the saucepan over a moderate heat, add the sliced cooked potatoes and give them a gentle but thorough mixing with the reserved onion oil to coat. After 2 or 3 minutes, drain the potatoes, once again reserving any excess oil.

3. Whisk the eggs in a bowl and stir in the potatoes and onions. Add salt and pepper to taste (I find ½ teaspoon of each is good).

4. Have a wooden spoon or spatula at the ready, plus a plate that fits over the frying pan. Then pour the reserved oil into a 20cm frying pan and set over a high heat (you may need to add some extra, fresh oil at this point – you want about 3 tablespoons in the pan). When the oil just starts to smoke, pour the tortilla mix into the pan, stirring for 10–20 seconds with a wooden spoon and moving the mix around the pan to distribute the cooked egg in among the runny until you have an egg/onion/potato mix that is approximately 20 percent cooked.

5. Give the pan a good levelling shake and leave the mix well alone to form a crust underneath, with the pan still on a high heat, for about 45 seconds. Check by lifting the tortilla slightly with the back of a spoon to see if the underside is going a nice golden brown. Turn the heat down low and continue to cook for another 2 minutes. The main body of the tortilla top should still be quite liquid, with only the sides well formed.

6. Remove the pan from the heat and place the plate over the frying pan. Using oven gloves or kitchen cloths to protect your hands, carefully invert the tortilla on to the plate, taking care not to spill any of the runny uncooked side.

7. Turn the heat to high again, then pour a little extra olive oil into the frying pan and slide the uncooked side of the tortilla back into the pan, tucking in the edges. Cook for another minute or so until golden brown in colour. The tortilla will be cooked if the middle feels sturdy but gives when you press it with your fingers. If it still feels a little too soft, continue to cook over a low heat until firmer. Remove from the pan and slide it on to a plate.

8. Allow the tortilla to cool before cutting into wedges and serving. Best eaten at room temperature.

PIPERADE

This dish of eggs ribboned with cooked onions and peppers, tomatoes and herbs features in the cookery books of stellar food writers such as Elizabeth David, Richard Olney and Keith Floyd, to name but a few. Piperade for me conjures up thoughts of brightest sunshine, long lunches and knocking back glasses of rosé in France all summer, some time in the 1970s. That said, I wasn't there, though I wish somehow I had been (I would have definitely worn a headscarf, big sunglasses and driven a tiny sports car).

~ ~ ~ ~

Serves 6

- 2 tbsp olive oil
- 100g thinly sliced
  prosciutto (optional)
- 2 medium white onions, diced
- 2 cloves of garlic, finely chopped
- 2 tbsp chopped fresh parsley
- 1 tbsp chopped fresh thyme leaves
- 1 bay leaf
- 2 red peppers, diced
- 2 green peppers, diced
- ½–1 tsp salt
- 6 medium tomatoes (fresh when
  ripe in summer, good-quality tinned
  at other times), peeled (see page 12),
  deseeded and chopped
- 1–1½ tsp chilli flakes or
  cayenne pepper
- 6 eggs

1. Put a large frying pan over a moderate heat and add 1 tablespoon of olive oil. Add the prosciutto (if using) and cook until golden and slightly crisped, about 3 minutes.

2. Remove to a plate with a slotted spoon and reserve. Keep any fat in the pan.

3. Return the pan to the heat with the rest of the oil. Add the onions and cook for 5 minutes, until soft and translucent, then add the garlic. Stir and cook for another 5 minutes or until very soft and the onions begin to turn golden brown. Add the herbs, diced peppers and salt.

4. Cover the pan with a lid and continue to cook over a low heat, stirring every now and then, until the peppers have softened, about 12 minutes.

5. Stir in the chopped tomatoes and chilli flakes (or cayenne pepper). Return the heat to moderate and cook uncovered for a further 10 or so minutes, until slightly thickened.

6. Now break the eggs into a bowl and lightly beat, then pour them into the pan. Lower the heat again and stir as if you were making scrambled eggs. With the egg just cooked, remove from the heat – the heat of the pan will continue to cook the eggs.

7. Serve topped with the fried prosciutto, if using.

EGG-FRIED BROWN RICE

A much-loved staple in our house. My eldest daughter and any grown-ups might arm themselves with a squeezy bottle of Sriracha chilli sauce to squirt here, there and everywhere.

~ ~ ~ ~

Serves 4
- 2 tbsp vegetable or sunflower oil
- 2 tbsp sesame oil
- 800g cold cooked brown rice
- 4 eggs
- salt
- 2 tbsp light soy sauce
- 1 tbsp fish sauce (optional)
- 200g defrosted frozen peas
- 6 spring onions, finely sliced

1. Heat the oils in a wok or large, deep frying pan on a high heat until it just starts to smoke, then add the rice and stir until well coated with the oil.
2. Cook over a high heat until all the rice is hot and some grains begin to crisp and stick to the bottom of the wok.
3. Beat the eggs with a pinch of salt.
4. Turn down the heat and add the beaten eggs, stirring well so that the egg mixture is fully absorbed by the rice, and turn up the heat again. Stir-fry for a couple of minutes, until the egg is cooked and well mixed in among the rice.
5. Add the soy and fish sauce (if using).
6. Stir in the peas and spring onions and serve straight away.

SWEETCORN
FRITTERS

'Mmmm, like pancakes with bits in!' So says four-year-old Ivy.

~ ~ ~ ~

Makes about 20 fritters
- 2 corn on the cob
- 3 eggs, separated
- 300ml buttermilk (or yoghurt thinned with milk)
- 100g medium-grade cornmeal or fine polenta
- 100g plain flour
- 1 tsp baking powder
- ½ tsp salt
- ¼ tsp freshly ground black pepper
- 1 tbsp melted butter
- oil for frying (sunflower/ vegetable/olive)

1. Cook the corn in boiling water for 8 minutes, until tender, then slice off the corn kernels and set aside.
2. Whisk the egg yolks into the buttermilk. Sift the dry ingredients in a large bowl, then make a well in the centre and pour in the buttermilk in a steady stream. Whisk until combined.
3. Add the cooked sweetcorn and the melted butter.
4. Whisk the egg whites in a large clean bowl until they form soft peaks. By hand is fine, using an electric whisk is faster and more fun for children.
5. Scoop and fold the egg whites into the sweetcorn batter.
6. When you're ready to eat, heat a non-stick frying pan with a spot of oil and blob spoonfuls (each about the size of a small orange) into the pan. Fry over a medium heat until golden brown. Flip with a spatula and repeat on the other side.
7. We eat these piping hot, with tomato ketchup. They would be equally nice with a herby mayonnaise (see opposite), and are great served with soured cream and sweet chilli sauce.

VARIATION: COURGETTE FRITTERS

You can substitute courgette for the corn if you like. Grate two courgettes, lightly salt and leave to drain in a colander for 10 minutes. Give the courgettes a good squeeze before adding them to the buttermilk mix as above.

BASIC
MAYONNAISE

Absolutely it is worth making your own.

~ ~ ~ ~

Makes 300ml
- 2 large, egg yolks
- salt and freshly ground black pepper
- ½ tsp Dijon mustard
- 2 tsp good white vinegar (wine or cider)
- 200ml sunflower oil, mixed with 100ml extra-virgin olive oil (you can use 300ml of just sunflower oil, but using extra-virgin olive oil by itself will overwhelm the mayonnaise)

1. Put the egg yolks, a pinch of salt, the mustard, vinegar and a little pepper into a mixing bowl and combine with a whisk.
2. Put the oils into a jug that is easy to pour from, then slowly start whisking a few drops of oil into the egg mix.
3. Very slowly increase the quantity of oil added each time, whisking in each addition so it is properly amalgamated before adding the next. Once the mayonnaise has started to hold its shape, add the oil in a thin stream, whisking continuously.
4. When you have added all the oil, you should have a thick and wobbly mayonnaise that holds its shape. Taste and check the seasoning and add a touch more vinegar if you like.
5. If you want to thin the mayonnaise, whisk in a few teaspoons of water.
6. Alternatively, you can use a food processor. Put the yolks, vinegar, mustard and seasoning into the bowl of the processor. Add the oil in a thin stream with the motor running, and proceed as for making by hand.

VARIATIONS

To brighten and lighten the mayonnaise, a spoon of crème fraîche or plain yoghurt mixed in can be a nice addition. To the finished mayonnaise add:

TARTARE SAUCE. 2 finely chopped hard-boiled eggs, 2 tablespoons of chopped fresh parsley, 3 finely chopped gherkins, 2 teaspoons of finely chopped capers and a squeeze of lemon juice.

ANCHOVY MAYONNAISE. Drained and puréed anchovies to taste, and add extra black pepper and lemon juice. About 4 anchovies to 150g of mayonnaise. Finely chopped fresh rosemary leaves work well with the anchovy.

AÏOLI. 1–3 finely puréed cloves of garlic to the other ingredients. Alternatively, boil the whole garlic cloves in water first for 2 or 3 minutes for a milder garlic flavour.

HERB MAYONNAISE. Finely chopped soft fresh herbs (dill, chives, tarragon, chervil or the feathery fronds of a fennel bulb would be my preference).

Note: If the mayonnaise splits, start again with fresh egg yolks. Pour the split mayonnaise into a jug, wipe out the bowl or food processor, add the new egg yolks and proceed as before using the split mayonnaise as per the original oil, adding it little by little.

WILD GARLIC FRITTATA

From late March to middling May, wild garlic is at its best and carpets many damp and shady woodland areas. With a broad, deep-green, triangular-stemmed leaf, wild garlic can also be identified by its mild garlic smell and dainty white flowers (young and tender wild garlic leaves are best, so pick them before the plant goes to seed and has too many white flowers). Pick only as many as you plan to use, stay clear of any areas frequented by dogs needing a wee, and if in any doubt as to what it is, don't pick it. Richard Mabey's *Food for Free* should put you on the right track for all things foraged.

Foraging with the children is fantastic. Nearer to the ground and with a competitive streak I find becoming in spirited kids, it never takes long before the required shopping bag is stuffed full.

The flavour of wild garlic is something akin to garlic, spinach and also spring onion. Verdant green, washed well and cooked in seconds, it is a versatile ingredient in the kitchen.

~ ~ ~ ~

Serves 4

- 250g chard or spinach leaves, washed and sliced into fat ribbons if the leaves are big, fine as they are if small
- 6 eggs
- 100g young wild garlic, washed and sliced into fat ribbons
- 75g Parmesan cheese, freshly grated
- 2 slices of day-old bread, crusts removed, soaked in 2–3 tbsp milk, squeezed dry and crumbled into wet breadcrumbs
- salt and freshly ground black pepper
- 1 tbsp vegetable oil

1. Preheat the oven to 180°C/gas mark 4. You will need a non-stick frying pan that is ovenproof and also small enough to fit in the oven.

2. Blanch the chard or spinach in a pan of boiling water for 1 minute or until just wilted. Drain, then squeeze out any excess water when cool enough to handle. Set aside.

3. Crack the eggs into a bowl and add the wild garlic, cooked and squeezed spinach or chard, Parmesan, soaked bread, salt and pepper into a bowl and mix together.

4. Heat your ovenproof frying pan over a high heat until the pan begins to just quiver with smoke, then add the vegetable oil.

5. Add the frittata mix to the pan and mix around for 10 or so seconds with a wooden spoon, then let the mixture settle and be brave enough to allow the frittata take on a nice colour underneath.

6. Place the pan in the oven and cook for 10–15 minutes, or until the egg is set and the frittata is ready.

7. Leave to cool in the pan for around 10 minutes, then turn out on to a plate. Best served warm and with a blob of mayonnaise (see page 53) alongside.

CURD

Make fruit curd at home. On toast and served with a cup of tea – I don't suppose there is a better breakfast. To sterilize jars, place freshly cleaned jam jars and lids in a warm oven (180°C/gas mark 4) for 10 minutes.

~ ~ ~ ~

Makes 2–3 jars

- 200ml juice from 5–6 large lemons (preferably unwaxed), plus the zest of 4, finely grated
- 250g caster sugar
- 100g unsalted butter, cut into cubes
- 2 eggs, plus 2 egg yolks

Lemon Curd

1. Put the lemon juice and zest, the sugar and the butter into a heatproof bowl set over a pan of just simmering water, making sure that the bottom of the bowl isn't touching the water. Stir with a whisk from time to time until the butter has melted.

2. Mix the eggs and egg yolks lightly with a whisk, then whisk into the lemon juice and melted butter mix. Whisk the curd over a gentle heat for 12–15 minutes, until it is thick enough to coat the back of a spoon, making sure you use a spatula from time to time to scrape down the sides of the bowl so that the curd gets evenly whisked over the heat.

3. Remove the bowl from the heat and stir occasionally as the mixture cools.

4. Store the curd in sterilized jars (see above) and seal. The curd will keep in the fridge, unopened, for up to 3 weeks. Use within 1 week once the jar has been opened.

5. You can pass the curd through a sieve if you find that it is not perfectly smooth.

Makes 2–3 jars

- 2 eggs, plus 3 egg yolks,
  beaten together
- 200ml blood orange juice, plus
  the zest from 2 blood oranges
- juice and zest of 1 lemon
  (preferably unwaxed)
- 100g unsalted butter, cut
  into cubes
- 80g caster sugar

Blood Orange Curd

1. Place the eggs, orange and lemon juice and zest, butter and sugar in a heatproof bowl set over a pan of simmering water, making sure that the bottom of the bowl doesn't touch the water. Stir continuously with a whisk for 12–15 minutes, until thick, making sure you scrape down the sides of the bowl.
2. Remove from the heat and let it cool a bit, stirring occasionally. Pour into sterilized jars and seal. The curd will keep for about 3 weeks in the fridge. Once opened, use within 1 week.
3. You can pass the curd through a sieve if you find that it's not perfectly smooth.

~ ~ ~ ~

Makes 2–3 jars

- 2 eggs, plus 2 egg yolks,
  beaten together
- 250ml passion fruit pulp, with ¾ of
  the seeds strained out (some seeds
  are nice, but too many and you'll
  have a crunchy curd!)
- 120g unsalted butter,
  cut into cubes
- 80g caster sugar

Passion Fruit Curd

1. Place the eggs, passion fruit pulp and remaining seeds, butter and sugar in a heatproof bowl set over a pan of just simmering water, making sure that the bottom of the bowl doesn't touch the water. Stir with a whisk from time to time until the butter has melted.
2. Whisk the curd over a gentle heat for 12–15 minutes, until it is thick enough to coat the back of a spoon, making sure you scrape down the sides of the bowl.
3. Remove from the heat and leave to cool a bit, stirring occasionally. Pour into sterilized jars and seal. The curd will keep for about 3 weeks in the refrigerator. Once opened, use within 1 week.
4. You can pass the curd through a sieve if you find that it's not perfectly smooth.

GRAINS

Cereals are a wonder. Not that supermarket aisle stacked floor to ceiling with lurid cardboard boxes; that place where cartoon bees, rainbow hoops and superheroes march past your eyeballs and on into your brain. Far more wholesome an image is the cereal fields where the grains are grown. These breezy fields of wheat, barley, corn, oats and more are a tremendous source for the store cupboard. Grains as a substitute for pasta, rice or potatoes are all incalculably useful.

Versatile in application and a natural companion to many different ingredients, cooking with grains is a great way to add texture and sustenance. Committed grain eaters will seek out those cereals not overly processed. So-called groats are the hulled kernels of the grain, with the nutritionally rich husk and bran portion left intact. Interesting, complex and nutty in flavour, groats give a reassuring bulk to soporific and seasonal stews and soups. Swollen in a sauce, these chewy, nubby whole grains are a marvel.

Used in summer, cooked grains flecked through robust salads are welcome respite from potatoes or pasta. Roast fennel and courgettes, with feta cheese and some farro or barley dressed with preserved lemons, chilli flakes, dill and olive oil, are delicious.

Polenta is also marvellous, a comfortable blanket of starch. From that molten bowl of buttery, cheesy cornmeal, fast-track to leftovers that you can spread flat and leave to solidify. Baked in the oven, slathered with a tomato sauce and strewn with fresh herbs and more cheese, polenta served like this is a fantastic alternative to pizza.

Come breakfast time, it's got to be oatmeal. Porridge is a contentious issue. Purists call for a porridge made only with oats, water and salt. I remember well breakfasts with my Scottish grandparents, when porridge was served throughout chilly summer holidays on the east coast. Piping hot, made with water and served with a knob of butter on top, it was decidedly salty and also the only time I was ever allowed to spoon sugar on to my breakfast all by myself. Quick as a flash went the spoon back to the sugar bowl without a grown-up noticing.

Making porridge for my own children, I like to use coarse rolled oats, preferring the texture they give to the finished porridge. I make porridge with half water and half milk, only adding a pinch of salt to mine after I've served theirs. And while I'm sure they'd love a little autonomy with the sugar bowl, I'm not convinced, and opt instead for a trickle of maple syrup or runny honey.

BARLEY BROTH

A staple and hearty bowlful during the winter months, this is the soup that can have everything and almost nothing. Use ham hock stock (see page 165) or chicken stock (see page 145), or just add water to the softened sweet sautéd vegetables when you add the barley. You can also add the shredded chicken or ham meat from the making of the stock if you like, or save this for another meal and just use the meat stock. As you like.

It is worth noting that this soup also eats better the day after it has been made, as the barley swells with the stock, making the grains more flavoursome. I like it too that the broth then becomes less soupy and more of a warm rubble of vegetable and grain.

~ ~ ~ ~

Serves 4, with leftovers

- 200g pearl or pot barley
- 2 tbsp olive oil
- 1 onion, diced
- 1 leek, washed and diced
- 2 sticks of celery, diced
- 2 carrots, peeled and diced
- 3 cloves of garlic, finely chopped
- 2 bay leaves
- 4 rashers of smoked streaky bacon, diced (optional, and not necessary if making a ham hock version)
- 1.2 litres hot chicken or ham hock stock (see pages 145 and 165 – with the chopped meat, if using)
- salt and freshly ground black pepper, to taste
- 1 small bunch of fresh parsley leaves, chopped, or 1 tbsp fresh thyme leaves or chopped fresh rosemary leaves

To serve

- olive oil
- freshly grated Parmesan cheese
- chilli flakes (optional)
- 4 lemon wedges (optional)

1. Soak the pearl barley (if using) in a bowl of water for 5 minutes. If using pot barley, soak overnight in cold water.

2. Place the barley in a pan and cover with plenty of cold water. Bring to the boil. Skim off any frothy residue that surfaces, then reduce the heat and simmer until cooked. Pot barley will take longer (50 minutes) than pearl (20–30 minutes).

3. Put the oil into a pan over a moderate heat. Add the onion and cook for a minute or two, until beginning to soften. Add the leek, celery, carrot, garlic and bay leaves. Add the bacon (if using). Sauté the vegetables and bacon for at least 20 minutes over a moderate/low heat, until soft and fragrant.

4. Add the cooked barley and the hot stock to the softened vegetables and bring to a simmer, then reduce the heat and cook for 5 minutes for the flavours to meld. If also using the meat from the making of the stock, add this to the pan, chopped or shredded into smallish pieces.

5. Season with salt and pepper, to taste. Add the herbs and stir.

6. Serve the broth in bowls, topped with a drizzle of olive oil, some grated Parmesan, a sprinkling of chilli flakes (if using) and with a lemon wedge to squeeze.

CABBAGE, BULGUR & ALLSPICE PILAF

Serves 4

- 2 onions, finely diced
- 75g butter
- 1 cinnamon stick
- 6 whole allspice, or tsp ground
- 200g spiced tomato sauce with cinnamon and allspice (see page 173)
- 300g bulgur wheat, soaked in water for 10 minutes and drained
- 1 small Hispi cabbage, cut into 6 wedges (still partially held together with the core), or another small crisp cabbage
- salt and freshly ground black pepper
- 800ml vegetable or chicken stock (see page 145), or water

To serve

- 50g sunflower seeds
- chilli flakes (optional)
- a small bunch of fresh mint, dill or parsley, chopped
- 200g plain yoghurt (I like to season mine with a pinch of salt)

1. Sauté the onions in half the butter in a wide pan over a medium-high heat for 2–3 minutes, stirring occasionally, until the onions have softened. Stir in the cinnamon, allspice and tomato sauce, followed by the drained bulgur wheat. Tip into a large bowl and let the flavours meld.

2. Return the pan to the heat and add the rest of the butter. When it is foaming add the cabbage wedges and a little salt and allow to colour a bit on each cut side, about 10 minutes in total.

3. Return the tomato-soaked bulgur wheat to the pan along with the stock and bring to the boil, then cover with a lid and simmer gently over a low heat for 15–20 minutes, until the bulgur and cabbage are tender and the stock has been absorbed. Taste and season with salt and pepper if necessary.

4. Meanwhile, toast the sunflower seeds in a dry frying pan until they are golden.

5. Serve the pilaf with the seeds, chilli flakes (if using) and herbs sprinkled on top, together with a spoonful of yoghurt.

SOFT POLENTA

Serves 4
- 450ml milk
- 450ml cold water
- salt and freshly ground black pepper
- 150g coarse polenta
- 50g Parmesan cheese, freshly grated
- 50g butter, diced

1. Pour the milk and water into a deep saucepan, add a little salt and bring to a simmer.
2. Pour the polenta into the simmering liquid in a thin stream, whisking all the time to ensure there are no lumps. Once the mixture gets too thick to whisk, change over to a wooden spoon.
3. Bring the polenta mix gently back to a simmer and cook, stirring constantly with the wooden spoon, for 5 minutes. Turn the heat down low and continue to cook gently for about 40 minutes, giving it a vigorous stir every couple of minutes.
4. Remove from the heat. Stir in the Parmesan and butter and season with salt and pepper, to taste.

~ ~ ~ ~

Fried Polenta

1. Make the basic polenta recipe, then pour into a shallow baking dish or roasting tray and chill.
2. Refrigerate for 2 hours. It will keep for a few days.
3. Remove the polenta from the dish and slice into pieces.
4. Heat a small amount of olive oil in a non-stick frying pan over a medium-high heat.
5. Add the polenta slices and cook until golden brown and crisp on both sides, about 8–10 minutes. Be careful, the polenta will splatter while frying.

~ ~ ~ ~

Baked Polenta

1. Use the basic polenta recipe, pour into a shallow baking dish or roasting tray and chill.
2. Refrigerate for 2 hours. It will keep for a few days.
3. Preheat the oven to 190°C/gas mark 5.
4. Slice the polenta, place on a lightly oiled baking sheet and dab with a few knobs of butter.
5. Bake for 20 minutes, until lightly browned and crisp.

FRIED HERRINGS WITH RHUBARB & BACON

Using oats to coat the herrings before frying them gives the fish a good robust crust and is a great alternative to batter. The sweet-sharp pickled rhubarb pairs beautifully with the oiliness of the fish.

~ ~ ~ ~

Serves 4

- 4 rashers of bacon or pancetta (optional)
- 1 tbsp oil, plus a little for the bacon (if using)
- 4 herring fillets
- salt and freshly ground black pepper
- Dijon mustard, for brushing the fish
- 120g rolled oats
- a knob of butter
- 4 generous tbsp pickled rhubarb, to serve (see page 244)

1. If using the bacon or pancetta, fry it in a pan with a little oil and reserve the fat for frying the herrings. Put the bacon aside to keep warm.

2. Season the herring fillets with salt and pepper and brush/ smear each side lightly with Dijon mustard.

3. Spread the oats on a plate and lay the herrings on top, pressing each side of the fillets firmly into the oats so they stick to the mustardy coating.

4. Heat a large, heavy-based frying pan over a medium heat. Add the oil and the reserved bacon fat, if using, and then put the coated fillets into the pan.

5. Fry for a minute on one side, then add the butter, turn the fillets over and fry for 1 or 2 minutes more, until the oat crust is golden and the fish is cooked through.

6. Serve straight away, with the bacon, if using, a spoonful of pickled rhubarb and another grind of black pepper.

TWO RIFFS ON FLAPJACKS

Flapjacks have a misleadingly healthy, socks-and-sandals sort of image. Bound by sugar and butter, they are anything but. Whizzed-up banana or pulpy cooked apple does much the same job to amalgamate the oats. These are quick to make and cheaper than buying those snack-style oaty bars. Thanks to Elly Curshen at The Pear Café for the second recipe, a riff on her banana and coconut flapjack recipe.

~ ~ ~ ~

Makes 12 flapjacks

- 400g Bramley apples, peeled, cored and chopped
- 200ml cold water
- 2 cinnamon sticks
- 200g rolled oats
- 60g soft light brown sugar (or as you like, for sweetness) or honey
- 80g raisins
- 1 tsp baking powder
- sunflower oil for greasing

Apple and cinnamon

1. Cook the apples to a pulp with the water and cinnamon over a moderate heat with a lid on the pan for about 8–10 minutes. Leave to cool.
2. Preheat the oven to 180°C/gas mark 4.
3. Mix the oats, sugar, raisins and baking powder in a bowl.
4. Add the apple pulp to the oats, removing the cinnamon sticks, and mix well.
5. Spoon into a greased 20 x 28cm baking tin, 5cm deep, and smooth out even and flat. Try not to have too many raisins poking out from the surface of the flapjack, as these tend to catch in the oven – poke them down with your forefinger.
6. Bake for 30–35 minutes, until nicely coloured and firm on top.
7. Leave to cool in the tin for 10 minutes before cutting into squares. Cool on a wire rack.

~ ~ ~ ~

Makes 12 flapjacks

- 3 tbsp sunflower oil, plus extra for greasing
- 200g jumbo oats
- 100g desiccated coconut
- 40g seeds (pumpkin, sunflower, poppy, linseed, sesame, etc.)
- a pinch of fine sea salt
- 100g chopped dates (cranberries, apricots, figs and raisins have also worked well)
- 4 very ripe medium bananas, peeled and sliced
- ½ tsp vanilla extract
- 3 tbsp olive oil

Banana and coconut

1. Preheat the oven to 180°C/gas mark 4.
2. Grease a 20 x 28cm baking tin, 5cm deep, with a little oil.
3. In a mixing bowl, mix the oats, coconut, seeds, salt and dates.
4. In a food processor or using a stick blender, mix the bananas, vanilla and oils into a smoothish paste.
5. Add the oat mix to the banana mix and combine well.
6. Pour into the baking tin, level the surface and bake for about 25 minutes until a nice golden brown and firm to touch.
7. Leave to cool in the tin for 10 minutes, then cut into squares. Cool on a wire rack.

BANANA & BUTTERMILK PANCAKES

Here the banana is whizzed up and mixed into the pancake batter. More like a fat pancake or – to give it its Kiwi name – a pikelet.

~ ~ ~ ~

Makes about 16 pancakes

- 150g spelt flour (you can use wholewheat or plain flour)
- 1 tbsp soft light brown sugar or honey
- a pinch of salt
- 1 tsp baking powder
- 1 tsp bicarbonate of soda
- 1 large extremely ripe banana, peeled
- 250ml buttermilk (or yoghurt thinned with milk)
- 1 egg
- 2 tbsp unsalted butter, plus extra for cooking the pancakes

1. In a medium bowl, whisk together all the dry ingredients. If using honey rather than sugar, add it in step 3 with all the other wet ingredients.

2. Slice the banana, put into a blender or food processor with the buttermilk and blend until completely puréed. Add the egg and butter and purée briefly on a low speed to bring everything together.

3. Pour the wet ingredients into the dry ingredients and whisk until everything just comes together to make a relatively smooth batter. If it seems a bit thick, add a bit more buttermilk.

4. Heat a non-stick frying pan over a low heat. These pancakes brown quite easily with the spelt flour and honey (if using), so don't let the pan get too hot. You'll need to cook them in batches.

5. Rub the pan with a bit of butter and dollop dessertspoon-size pancakes into the pan. Space them well apart, as they will spread a bit. Turn the heat up a little.

6. When bubbles start to appear in the centre of the pancakes, gently lift the edge to see how well they are coloured underneath.

7. If you are happy with the colour, flip them over very carefully and cook for a couple of minutes until just done. Remove the cooked pancakes to a plate while you cook more, and wipe out the pan with kitchen paper if the butter has burnt at all.

8. Serve the pancakes as soon as possible, keeping them warm on a covered plate in a low oven while you cook the others. Especially nice with Greek yoghurt and extra honey or maple syrup. Unused batter will keep in the fridge for a few hours.

9. These pancakes can be reheated in little stacks, sprinkled with sugar, in a hot oven if you have any left over – which is unlikely.

BIRCHER
MUESLI

Also called 'overnight oats', the oats are soaked overnight in apple juice (I like to use a half/half dilution with water to reduce the sugar levels of using all juice). A brilliant summery version of porridge – a bowl of Bircher and it's off to school they go. Come the colder mornings, we'll no doubt switch back to porridge.

~ ~ ~ ~

Serves 4
- 400g rolled oats
- 700ml apple juice (or ½ apple juice/½ water dilution)
- 2 eating apples
- plain Greek yoghurt, to serve
- honey or maple syrup, to sweeten (optional)

1. Place the oats in a bowl and pour the liquid over the top. Cover and place in the fridge for a couple of hours minimum – overnight is best.
2. When ready to serve, grate the apples into the oats and stir until well combined.
3. Serve in bowls, adding a spoonful of yoghurt and stirring well. Add the honey or maple syrup, if using, and stir again.
4. The Bircher will keep very well in the fridge for up to 3 days.

VARIATIONS

Fresh fruit, dried fruit, seeds, nuts or flavoured yoghurt can all be added.

PULSES

Were it not for pulses, my cooking would be curtailed and my store cupboard would be embarrassingly bare. A vegetarian as a teenager, and later a student with indeterminate numbers of hungry, thirsty flatmates for supper, it was during these years that I learnt to cook pulses well and with panache.

A pulse is the seed within a pod that is dried for culinary use. Traffic-light shades of red, orange and green, lentils find numerous different uses in my cooking. I am fickle in my favouritism: to Italy and a salad with herbs and olive oil, the Middle East to scoop, dressed with yoghurt, lemony sumac and browned butter, then on into India, punchy with ginger and chilli for a dhal. Lentils are cheap and easy to come by.

There are a few high-falutin' lentils: Puy, Castelluccio, Pardina and Black Beluga all find favour with chefs for their fine texture, meaty flavour and the fact that they retain their shape so well when cooked. While certainly delicious, they are also more expensive.

It is just as well then, particularly when cooking for children, that lentils need not especially retain their shape in soups, dhals and such. Take a bow, humble lentil, and salute that stick blender of yours. With no need to soak, it is still a good idea to give lentils a quick sluicing in cold running water to wash away any starchy dust.

Beans, likewise, may find themselves in use depending on the spices, herbs and other ingredients such as lemons that I have to hand at any given moment. Pearly white cannellini, speckled borlotti and creamy, gnarly chickpeas are among my favourites.

Above all, what I like about dried beans is the forethought that cooking them requires. I like that you have to remember to soak the beans overnight, leaving them to plump up in a bowl of cold water as you go about your day. Cheating (bringing them to the boil, leaving to them to cool, then discarding the water and bringing to the boil again to begin the cooking process) never feels quite right, but needs must and all that.

My children love food that has a pulse. Forgive me. In essence, pulses are a vehicle for flavour. And children love flavourful food.

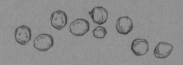

CATCH-ALL
LENTIL SOUP

A good soup can surely hide a thousand vegetables. Thereabouts. It doesn't especially matter which for my children, as long as the resulting liquid is a particular shade of orange. I have experimented with green (broccoli), brown (onion) and even yellow (sweetcorn) soups before, but it is only so-called 'orange soup' that cuts the mustard in our house.

The best advice I can give for soup-making is to let the vegetables soften and sauté in the pan for as long as possible, turning soft, melting and sweet. Don't be tempted to hurry the process. You want the vegetables to cook until absolutely soft and golden, almost caramelized, as these will be the backbone of the soup and offer depth and sweetness. Don't add any liquid until you have yourself a nice soffritto, as the Italians call this mixture.

~ ~ ~ ~

Serves 4
- 250g red lentils
- 2 tbsp olive oil
- 2 medium onions, diced
- 2 carrots, peeled and diced
- 2 celery sticks, diced
- 3 cloves of garlic, chopped
- 1 tsp each coriander and cumin seeds, ground and toasted (see page 12)
- ½ x 400g tin of tomatoes, or the juice from a whole tin of tomatoes
- salt and either freshly ground black pepper or chilli flakes

To serve
- hazelnut dukkah (see opposite)
- plain Greek yoghurt (optional)

1. Rinse the lentils under cold running water for a minute, or soak in a big bowl with plenty of cold water for 5 minutes, then drain.

2. Heat the oil in a heavy-bottomed pan over a moderate heat and add the onions. Cook until soft and translucent – at least 5–10 minutes.

3. Add the carrots, celery and garlic and continue to cook over a moderate/low heat until the vegetables are completely soft and have begun to turn an ever so slightly nutty golden brown – at least 15–20 minutes. The mix should smell rich and delicious. Add the toasted spices and stir for an extra minute or two.

4. Add the drained lentils and the tomatoes and bring to the boil. Add enough cold water to just cover the ingredients in the pan and cook for 20–30 minutes. After this time the lentils should have collapsed and the sharpness of the tomatoes should have abated. You may need to add more water, depending on the consistency you're after.

5. For a completely smooth soup, tip the lentils into a blender and blitz. If you would rather, you can reserve about one-third of the soup unblitzed for extra texture and mix the two together. Add salt and pepper or chilli flakes, to taste.

6. Serve with hazelnut dukkah (see opposite) and a dollop of Greek yoghurt if you like.

DUKKAH

This brilliant Middle Eastern ground spiced nut mix doesn't involve pulses, but it goes brilliantly with the catch-all lentil soup (see opposite). Dukkah is often served with extra-virgin olive oil as a dipping condiment for bread or sprinkled over salads. It will keep perfectly well for up to a month in a sealed jar, to be used as and when.

~ ~ ~ ~

Makes 1 jar

- 110g hazelnuts (walnuts or almonds would be good too)
- 2 tbsp coriander seeds
- 2 tbsp cumin seeds
- 1 tsp flaked sea salt (e.g. Maldon)
- freshly ground black pepper

1. Preheat the oven to 160°C/gas mark 3. Spread the hazelnuts evenly on a baking tray and roast until nicely toasted and golden brown – 10–15 minutes.

2. If your hazelnuts have skins, then while they're still hot, over a kitchen bin tip the nuts into deep-sided colander and work them around and around with a wooden spoon, or use your hands if the nuts are cool enough. You will find the rough skin easily flakes and falls off through the holes of the colander. (Though I am minded to think a bit of hazelnut skin never hurt anyone.)

3. Use a food processor, or a pestle and mortar, or wrap the nuts in a tea towel and bash them with a rolling pin, to crush the nuts to a coarse consistency.

4. Meanwhile, toast the whole coriander and cumin in a dry pan in the oven at the same time as your nuts, for 5 or so minutes – until they begin to smell and crackle. Grind them with a pestle and mortar or in a spice grinder.

5. Mix the toasted nuts and spices together with the salt and a grind of pepper and store in a screw-top jar.

SYRIAN LENTIL 'SOUP'

I first had this thick soup cooked for me by a chef friend who worked in London's Moro restaurant. Earthy bold lentils made piquant with coriander, yoghurt and lemon, this is just one of the many ways my kids will wolf them down.

~ ~ ~ ~

Makes 4
- 300g lentils (green or brown)
- 3 medium onions, finely sliced
- 3 tbsp olive oil, plus extra to serve
- 4 cloves of garlic, finely sliced
- 3 heaped tsp cumin seeds, toasted and ground (see page 12)
- a large bunch of fresh coriander (stalks and leaves separated)
- 1.75 litres cold water
- 4 tbsp Greek yoghurt
- ½ a clove of garlic, crushed
- salt
- juice of ½ a lemon
- chilli flakes

1. Soak the lentils in a bowl of cold water, rinsing them several times to remove any dirt or grit.

2. Over a moderate heat, cook the onions in the oil for a good 10 minutes. You want them soft and beginning to turn golden.

3. Add the garlic and toasted cumin and continue to fry over a moderate heat for another couple of minutes.

4. Add the coriander stalks and the water, or enough to more than cover the lentil mix. Turn up the heat and bring to the boil. Skim off any froth that surfaces. Turn the temperature down and continue to cook at a moderate bubble for about 30 minutes, watching the water level – you can always top it up a little if you need to.

5. While the lentils are cooking, mix the yoghurt with the crushed garlic and a pinch of salt.

6. When the lentils are ready, take them off the heat. You want the individual lentils to be completely squishable between two fingers and the whole to be a soupy mass.

7. Taste the lentils and add salt as needed. Add the lemon juice.

8. Serve the lentils in bowls and to each add a spoonful of seasoned yoghurt, some coriander leaves, a sprinkle of chilli flakes and a spoonful of olive oil.

9. We like to eat this with warm flatbreads, to mop up the lentils.

COCONUT DHAL

I think I could just about make a dhal with my eyes closed. Here is my version of the dish in its simplest form. Tamarind paste, tinned tomatoes, fresh tomatoes, frozen peas, spinach leaves and grated fresh coconut have all made guest appearances in this recipe over time. I don't add chilli to my dhal, preferring that everyone spice their own bowlful with pickles accordingly. Serve with carrot and mint raita (see opposite), plain rice or flatbreads, and Indian jarred pickles and chutneys.

~ ~ ~ ~

Serves 4

- 250g red lentils
- 1.2 litres cold water
- 1 cinnamon stick
- 1 level tsp turmeric
- 200ml coconut milk
  (½ a 400ml tin)
- salt
- 3 tbsp vegetable oil
- 1 large white onion, finely diced
- 3 cloves of garlic, finely sliced
- 1 thumb-size piece of unpeeled
  fresh root ginger, grated
- 1 level tsp garam masala
- 1 tsp each cumin and coriander seeds,
  toasted and ground (see page 12)
- 2 tsp mustard seeds
- 15 or so curry leaves (I buy mine
  fresh in bulk and freeze them)
- 2 plum tomatoes, peeled (see page 12),
  or tinned, or the juice from one tin

1. Give the lentils a good rinse in plenty of cold water to get rid of any starchy dust that would make the dhal gluey.

2. Put the lentils into a large saucepan with the water, cinnamon stick and turmeric, give a thorough stir and bring to the boil. Skim off any froth that surfaces and simmer for 30 minutes, until the lentils are cooked through and have fallen apart.

3. Add the coconut milk and a little salt. Do not let this mixture boil – the coconut will curdle if this happens. Continue to cook for a further 15 minutes, until the dhal has thickened but remains soupy. Take the pan off the heat.

4. Meanwhile, put the oil into a frying pan over a moderate heat and fry the onion until soft and beginning to turn golden brown – about 10 minutes. Add the garlic and grated ginger and continue to fry for a further 3 minutes or so.

5. Add the toasted spices, mustard seeds and curry leaves, put a lid on the pan and gently fry until the mustard seeds have stopped jumping about and crackling. Add the tomatoes (or tomato juice) and cook for about 5 minutes, until broken down and mixed well with the spices.

6. Add the spiced onion tomato mix to the dhal, stir well and check the seasoning.

CARROT & MINT RAITA

Okay, not a pulse but indispensable with the coconut dhal, opposite.

~ ~ ~ ~

Makes 200g

- 1 carrot, peeled and grated
- 3 spring onions, finely sliced
- 200ml plain yoghurt
- 1 lime
- ½ a clove of garlic, crushed
- 1 small bunch of mint, leaves picked and roughly chopped
- salt and freshly ground black pepper

1. Combine the carrot and spring onions in a bowl with the yoghurt.
2. Squeeze in the lime juice and add the garlic and chopped mint leaves.
3. Season with salt and pepper.

~ ~ ~ ~ ~ ~ ~ ~ ~ ~ ~ ~

BAKED BEANS

We like baked beans. But I cannot bear the tinned sort. Much too sweet and flabby in the mouth. Homemade baked beans are a world away.

~ ~ ~ ~

Serves 4

- 250g dried cannellini beans, soaked in cold water overnight or for at least 8 hours
- 2 bay leaves (optional)
- 1 clove of garlic (optional)
- 1 recipe of tomato sauce with sage (see page 173)
- salt and freshly ground black pepper
- olive oil

1. Drain and rinse your soaked beans and place them in a large saucepan with plenty of fresh water. (A couple of bay leaves and a clove of garlic added with the water wouldn't go amiss at this point.)
2. Bring to the boil and skim off any froth, then reduce the heat to a simmer. They should take anything between 1 and 1½ hours. You want the beans easily squashable between your fingers. There's nothing worse than undercooked beans – they can be horribly chalky.
3. Once the beans are cooked, drain them and add them to the tomato sauce. Go easy adding the beans, as you don't want to run out of sauce. Season with salt and pepper, and stir in a tablespoon of olive oil for good measure.

BEAN & BROCCOLI SOUP

Serves 4

- 200g dried cannellini beans, soaked in cold water overnight or for at least 8 hours
- 1 leek, washed, green part kept whole, white part chopped
- 4 celery sticks, one kept whole, the rest chopped
- 1 bay leaf
- 1 tsp salt
- 2 tbsp olive oil, plus extra to serve
- 1 medium onion, diced
- 1 clove of garlic, chopped
- 1 tbsp chopped rosemary leaves
- ½ a lemon (optional)
- 1 head of broccoli, broken into little florets
- freshly ground black pepper

To serve

- 4 tbsp freshly grated Parmesan cheese
- chilli flakes (optional)

1. Drain the soaked beans and put them into a large saucepan with the green part of the leek and the whole celery stick, the bay leaf and plenty of cold water. Bring to the boil, then skim off any froth and simmer the beans until they are cooked. This should take about 1–1½ hours. You want the beans to be completely tender. Towards the last 10 minutes of the cooking time, add ½ teaspoon of salt to the water.

2. When the beans are cooked, remove from the heat and leave to cool in a bowl or other container, still in their liquid. Discard the bay leaf, leek and celery.

3. Return the pan to a moderate heat and add the olive oil. Add the onions, garlic and rosemary, the remaining ½ teaspoon of salt, and the chopped leeks and celery, and cook for 10 minutes, until the vegetables are softened but not browned.

4. Put the cooked beans back into the pan, add enough of their liquid to cover completely and simmer for 10 minutes.

5. Place the beans and liquid in a blender and blitz until smooth. Check the seasoning – you may want to squeeze a little lemon juice into the soup at this point.

6. Bring a pan of water to the boil, add the broccoli florets and boil for 3–5 minutes, until cooked. Drain.

7. Warm the bean soup in the pan and add the broccoli. Stir and check the seasoning.

8. Serve in bowls, with grated Parmesan, a slick of olive oil and a sprinkling of chilli flakes, if using.

VARIATION

For a non-vegetarian version, stir through 8 chopped anchovy fillets when warming the soup and broccoli in the pan.

CASSOULET

Meaty beans. The origins of cassoulet lie in the rustic cooking of south-west France. The dish can be as simplified or as rarefied as you like. Any which way, it must always contain beans (haricot are best) and meat. Use black beans and you're on track for a Brazilian feijoada.

~ ~ ~ ~

Serves 4, with seconds

For the basic beans
- 400g dried white haricot beans, soaked in cold water overnight
- 1 onion, peeled
- 1 carrot, peeled
- 1 piece of bacon rind (see below)
- 2 bay leaves
- 2 cloves of garlic, peeled and left whole
- salt and freshly ground black pepper

For the meats and cassoulet
- 2 onions
- 4 cloves of garlic
- 4 tbsp duck fat, from the confit duck legs (see below)
- 2 whole tinned tomatoes, drained of juice and roughly chopped
- 3 bay leaves
- 200g bacon, in one piece, skin removed and reserved (for beans, see above)
- 2 confit duck legs (see page 147), cut into pieces
- 4 large garlicky sausages (Toulouse and with highest possible meat content are best), cut into 4 pieces
- 3 tbsp breadcrumbs

1. To cook the beans, first drain them and put them into a large pan with the onion, carrot, bacon rind, bay leaves and garlic. Cover with water and bring to the boil, skimming off any froth that appears on the surface. Turn the heat down to a simmer, then cook for 40 minutes to 1 hour (depending how old they are) until the beans are almost tender. Towards the last 10 minutes of the cooking time, add ½ teaspoon of salt to the water. Drain the beans, keeping the cooking liquid and discarding the flavourings.

2. Preheat the oven to 140°C/gas mark 1.

3. Slice the onions and garlic and soften in a pan in half the duck fat, then add the tomatoes along with the bay leaves. Cook for about 20 minutes until sticky and rich. Check for seasoning, then put to one side.

4. Cut the bacon piece into thick strips and gently brown in the remaining duck fat for a few minutes together with the duck legs and the sausages – you are just giving these meats colour, not cooking them, as they will go on to cook in the braising process. Gently stir in the onion and tomato mix.

5. Lay half the meat mix in the bottom of a deep earthenware or enamelled cast-iron casserole dish and cover with some of the beans. Add another layer of the meat, then another layer of beans. Top up with some of the reserved cooking liquid from the beans, to just cover.

6. Top with half the breadcrumbs and cook in the oven for 1 hour, then break the crust that has formed and stir it back into the cassoulet. Top once more with the remaining crumbs and return the dish to the oven for a further hour, until the crust is formed again and golden.

7. Serve the cassoulet with a great big green salad dressed sharply with red wine vinegar, a little olive oil and some salt and pepper.

ROASTED CRISP CHICKPEAS

Serve these as a snack, or scattergun over a turlu turlu (see page 177) or a big bowl of hummus (see below).

~ ~ ~ ~

Makes a bowlful

- 1 x 400g tin of chickpeas
- 3 tbsp olive oil
- 1 tsp each cumin and coriander seeds, ground and toasted (see page 12)
- ½–1 tsp chilli flakes, to taste
- salt, to taste

1. Heat the oven to 200°C/gas mark 6.
2. Drain the chickpeas as much as possible, patting them dry with kitchen paper or a clean tea towel.
3. Place them in an baking tray big enough to take them in a single layer, and toss with the olive oil to coat.
4. Add the spices and salt and roast until golden brown and crisp – about 15 minutes.
5. Check the seasoning and serve immediately.

~ ~ ~ ~ ~ ~ ~ ~ ~ ~

HUMMUS

My children have an insatiable appetite for hummus. The trick to getting it like the shop-bought stuff is to blend the chickpeas with cold water and only use olive oil to dress the finished hummus.

~ ~ ~ ~

Makes a good bowlful

- 1 tin of chickpeas or 2 cups of roasted chickpeas (see above)
- 150g light tahini paste
- juice of ½ a small lemon
- 1 clove of garlic, crushed
- salt, to taste
- extra-virgin olive oil, to serve

1. Drain the chickpeas and put them into a food processor along with the tahini, lemon juice, garlic and salt. Process until the chickpeas are broken down and all is well mixed.
2. With the motor still running, add cold water bit by bit until you reach the desired consistency. I like mine to drop off the back of a spoon like whipped double cream.
3. Store the hummus in a covered bowl or tub. If not using straight away, it will keep for up to 3 days in the fridge.
4. To serve, give the hummus a generous slick of olive oil.

Note: Ground sumac, black onion seeds and roasted chickpeas are all good decorative additions to a bowl of hummus and go some way to making its very beigeness a perfect backdrop.

SPRING ONION FARINATA

Farinata is a speciality from Liguria, in Italy. Chickpea (gram) flour can be found in many Asian and Indian shops. My version of farinata is thin and crisp, more like a pancake, with fried spring onions added to the mix. Herbs are also nice in the batter – harder varieties like rosemary, sage and thyme hold their own better on contact with the hot pan. A non-stick frying pan and a wide flexible spatula make flipping the farinata much easier.

~ ~ ~ ~

Makes about five 20cm farinatas

- 125g chickpea (gram) flour
- 225g cold water
- sea salt
- 2 tbsp olive oil, plus more for frying
- 1 bunch of spring onions

1. In a bowl positioned on the digital scales, weigh out the chickpea flour, then zero the scales and weigh in the water. This is the easiest and most accurate method.

2. Add ¼ teaspoon of salt and the olive oil and give the batter a good whisk. Cover and let the mix stand for at least 1 hour at room temperature. Bubbles and froth will surface during that time. This is fine; it just means the batter is working.

3. When ready to cook, slice the spring onions and add them to the batter.

4. Heat a frying pan over a high heat. Add a good spoonful of olive oil to the pan, then add a ladleful of the batter. Swirl it to the edges of the pan as if making a pancake.

5. When bubbles start to appear on the surface of the farinata, carefully flip it over. It should be golden and flecked with brown.

6. Cook the second side until it is the same colour, adding a little more oil to the underside of the farinata if needed to stop it from scorching.

7. When cooked, remove from the pan and place on a plate, sprinkling with salt to taste. Serve immediately.

Note: My favourite way to eat farinata is hot from the pan, topped with rocket leaves, torn soft cheese (mozzarella, or you could use feta or ricotta), plenty of lemon squeezed over and a slick of olive oil. Add salt, pepper or chilli flakes to taste. Think of it as a flavoursome pizza base – and experiment. Cooked green beans dressed with lemon, olive oil, mint and lots of grated Parmesan would be fantastic. Likewise, squashed courgettes (see page 179) piled on top with mozzarella or Parmesan are great.

PANISSE
(ROSEMARY & CHILLI)

Panisse is a traditional Italian street food. Crunchy, gnarled and gnobbled, these bite-size pieces of fried chickpea batter are a moreish snack. The unfried panisse will keep well in the fridge for a couple of days, but it might release a bit of water, so change the container every day, and fry when needed.

~ ~ ~ ~

Makes enough for a couple of bowlfuls
- 150g chickpea (gram) flour
- 500ml water
- salt and freshly ground black pepper (optional)
- 1 tbsp chopped fresh rosemary leaves
- chilli flakes, to taste (about ½ tsp does the trick)
- sunflower or vegetable oil, for frying

1. Sift the chickpea flour into a pan and whisk in the cold water gradually to avoid lumps. Add ½ teaspoon of salt, the chopped rosemary and chilli flakes to taste.

2. Place over a moderately high heat, mixing continuously with a whisk until the mixture thickens and starts to bubble. Once it does, switch to a wooden spoon, turn the heat to low and cook, stirring continuously, for another 10 minutes.

3. Spread the mixture on a 28 x 20cm baking tray to a depth of about 1–2 cm, roughing up the surface as you go – this will give the broken pieces of panisse a good rubbly texture when fried. Leave to stand for 1 hour.

4. When ready to fry the panisse, roughly break it into thumb-size nuggets.

5. Heat some oil in a large, deep pan (the oil should be at least 5cm deep) over a moderately high heat until approximately 180°C. If you don't have a thermometer, drop a cube of bread into the hot oil and it should fry golden brown in 60 seconds. Fry the panisse in small batches until golden all over – about 1–1½ minutes.

6. Drain on kitchen paper. Sprinkle with extra salt as you wish, extra chilli flakes and/or black pepper.

PASTA, DUMPLINGS & NOODLES

Home from a holiday and with next to nothing in the cupboard, pasta is the miracle meal that can take just ten minutes. Spaghetti with tomato sauce has been my emergency supper more times than I can count.

In the time it takes to cook the spaghetti, I'll have made the sauce. If I am feeling particularly athletic, I might nip outside for a spot of metropolitan rosemary foraging. Thank you to all those homeowners whose rosemary bushes spill out and on to pavement space; I take the tiniest sprig and only from the really bushy plants. In time, and with greener fingers, I will plant my own, I promise. Chilli flakes (I like Turkish Aleppo or Urfa for their subtle, sweet, hot hit) are a staple in my kitchen. In fact, I often use them in lieu of black pepper. as does my eldest, Grace, who enjoys their fruity punch. And a fridge lacking a lump of Parmesan puts me in a panic. With a few simple additions like these, pasta is a reliable and brilliant fast food.

At home, we have a shelf weighed down with the stuff, all blue and yellow packets in various states of undress. It's a sorry day when two packets of a different pasta shape get jostled into a boiling pan to make the one supper. No real matter, as long as they share a cooking time.

Pasta, such an easy meal to cook, but noodles are even quicker. My children love them. It is quite possibly the only meal where slurping with a noisy 'schawwwp!' as strand reaches mouth is allowed. My kids have infant chopsticks where the two sticks are stuck together at the top like a pair of giant tweezers. After a quick pre-dinner sword-fight, these chopsticks are great not only for eating the noodles but also for helping children get to grips with the more grown-up version.

Dumpling. Onomatopoeic is the dimply-skinned dumpling. My stepmother is Chinese and makes terrific dumplings known as jiaozi. Try as I might, I cannot make these to her exacting standard. With dextrous fingers that pinch and fold at a pace, hers are the perfect dumplings to dip in soy sauce, black malt vinegar and chilli oil. It is with mirth and affection that she sends us off home with a bag of her freshly made dumplings. 'A cook, and she can't fold a dumpling seam,' she fondly tsk-tsks.

Thankfully there is another way with dumplings, should your rolling and folding skills not pass muster. Gnocchi, dumplings by any other name, are great fun to make with children, and I've yet to meet a child who doesn't like them. Spaetzle, German/Austrian in origin, are made with a dumpling batter pushed through the holes of a colander with a spatula into fast-boiling water. Cooked and cooled, these teardrop-shaped dumplings are then fried in a sauté pan. Miraculously, they puff up, crisp, golden and addictive.

It is worth noting when cooking pasta that different pasta shapes share affinity with different sauces. Those with a large surface area and simple form respond well to lighter sauces with little texture to them. Chunkier sauces that haven't been over-blitzed or processed work better with more robust pasta shapes that provide crevices and pockets for the sauce to nestle in. Hit on the right combination of pasta and sauce, and you'll really notice the difference in the finished dish.

GREEN PEA PESTO

If I never see another jar of pesto it will be too soon. I can appreciate the speed and ease of boiling pasta and spooning sauce from a jar, but jarred pesto sauces are too salty and give little in the way of nutritional value.

Pesto in a jar has hijacked the supermarket shelves and home fridges of a generation. There is another way. Pesto doesn't have to be made with basil – and purists who insist otherwise, I say, 'More fool, you.'

In the time it takes for the pasta to cook, depending on shape, the following pesto recipe can be made from scratch.

~ ~ ~ ~

Serves 4
- 400g defrosted frozen peas
- 100g crème fraîche
- 1 small bunch of fresh mint, leaves roughly chopped
- ¼–½ clove of garlic, crushed (to taste, remembering raw garlic is quite pervasive)
- a squeeze of lemon juice
- 1 tbsp extra-virgin olive oil
- a handful of freshly grated Parmesan cheese, plus extra to serve
- salt and freshly ground black pepper
- 300g dried pasta (orecchiette or conchiglie would be my preference here)

1. Pour the peas into a wide, shallow bowl and cover with boiling water.
2. Drain the peas once softened. They don't need to be hot.
3. In a blender, or using a stick blender, blitz the peas with the crème fraîche, mint leaves, garlic, lemon and olive oil. Pulse the mix – it is nice to have a bit of pea texture and for it not to be too homogenous. Alternatively, reserve about a third of the frozen peas and add them whole to the whizzed mass.
4. Once blitzed to the desired consistency, stir in the grated Parmesan and season with salt and pepper.
5. Cook the pasta according to the packet instructions. Drain.
6. Put the pea sauce into the pasta pan and stir over a moderate heat for 30 or so seconds, to take the chill off. Add the cooked pasta, mix well and serve in bowls, with extra Parmesan.

PASTA WITH NETTLE PESTO

Nettles are delicious and, despite their reputation for giving you a nasty sting, surprisingly foolproof to pick. Arming yourself with a pair of washing-up gloves, pick only the first four leaves down from the top of the plant and in an area free of car fumes (and especially any dogs in need of a wee).

Once cooked, the nettles lose their sting and taste like fragrant lemony spinach. They are best eaten in early spring and autumn, when the plant has new growth and the leaves are tender. Don't use nettles once the plant has flowered, as the leaves can become bitter (and, some say, toxic).

It might just be that your back garden has the perfect patch of bright young nettles. To harvest nettles at their best all year round, you can strim a nettle patch back, forcing it to make continual growth so that you can pick the new leaves as they appear.

~ ~ ~ ~

Serves 4

- salt and freshly ground black pepper
- 100g young nettles (roughly 3 tightly packed cups)
- 1 clove of garlic, crushed to a paste with a little salt
- 50g pine nuts, toasted, or untoasted walnuts (so as to keep them soft)
- 120ml extra-virgin olive oil
- 20g Parmesan cheese, freshly grated, to taste
- 300g dried pasta (spaghetti, linguine or farfalle would be my preference here)

1. Find a pan large enough to take the nettles and fill it three-quarters full with water. Bring to the boil and add salt.

2. Have a bowl filled with iced water at the ready.

3. Using tongs or gloves, pick over the nettles, discarding any stalks, and wash well.

4. Add the nettles to the salted boiling water, cook for 2 minutes, then drain immediately.

5. Place the nettles in the bowl of iced water to arrest the cooking process. When cool, drain them and squeeze dry inside a clean tea towel to remove as much moisture as you can. Coarsely chop them on a board.

6. Put the cooked nettles into a food processor along with the garlic and pine nuts. With the machine on a low speed, slowly add the olive oil. Season to taste with salt, pepper and Parmesan. Alternatively, you can grind the nettles, pine nuts, garlic and Parmesan cheese to a paste using a pestle and mortar, then slowly incorporate the oil.

7. Cook the pasta according to the packet instructions and combine with the nettle pesto, reserving and using a little of the pasta cooking water to loosen the mixture if needed.

PASTA WITH SAUSAGE, CHILLI & NUTMEG

This sauce is also good served with polenta (see page 65).

~ ~ ~ ~

Serves 4

- 3 large coarse pork sausages (100 percent meat)
- 1 tbsp olive oil
- ½ an onion, finely diced
- 2 cloves of garlic, crushed
- 1 x 400g tin of tomatoes, well drained and chopped
- a pinch of chilli flakes
- 300g dried pasta (tube-like shapes such as penne, rigatoni or tortiglioni would be my preference here)
- 100ml double cream
- ¼ or ⅓ of a nutmeg, freshly grated
- salt and freshly ground black pepper
- freshly grated Parmesan cheese, to serve

1. Slice the sausages lengthways and remove the skins. Roughly chop the sausage meat filling.

2. In a heavy-bottomed saucepan, heat the olive oil and cook the onions until soft – 5–8 minutes.

3. Add the sausage meat and cook for 5 minutes until lightly browned, breaking up the meat with the back of a spoon as it cooks.

4. Next add the garlic and cook for another minute or two, until fragrant.

5. Add the tomatoes and chilli flakes, stir well and lower the heat. Cook gently for about 10 minutes, stirring and scraping every now and then.

6. Meanwhile, cook the pasta according to the packet instructions.

7. Add the cream to the sauce, heat without letting it boil, and check the seasoning, adding nutmeg, salt and pepper to taste.

8. Stir in the cooked pasta, adding a little of the pasta cooking water if you need to loosen it, and serve topped with freshly grated Parmesan.

BROCCOLI PESTO PASTA

Cooking the broccoli in the same pot as the pasta and for practically the same amount of time results in the broccoli almost entirely breaking up during cooking. I am always surprised by just how much broccoli I can pack into my children when I make this for their tea. Green-flecked and almost creamy, the broccoli coats the pasta and combines beautifully with the garlic, rosemary and olive oil. Twelve minutes, from a standing start with the water already boiling, I can have this supper on the table. Tick-tick-tick.

~ ~ ~ ~

Serves 4

- 300g dried pasta
  (penne or spaghetti would be
  my preference here)
- salt
- 350g broccoli head (broken down
  into smallish florets each the size
  of a ping-pong ball – some of the
  whiter inner stalk is fine to leave on)
- 3 tbsp olive oil
- 3 cloves of garlic, chopped finely
- 1 tbsp chopped fresh rosemary leaves
- juice of ½–1 lemon
- chilli flakes (optional)
- a handful of grated Parmesan
  cheese, plus extra to serve

1. Bring a large pan of water to the boil, adding salt if you wish. Add the pasta and bring back to the boil. Tip in the broccoli florets and cook the whole lot according to the pasta packet instructions. The broccoli will overcook. You want this to happen.

2. When the pasta is cooked, drain the pasta and broccoli into a colander.

3. Using the same pan, return it to a moderate heat and add 2 tablespoons of the olive oil. Add the chopped garlic and sauté for a minute. Don't let it brown. Add the chopped rosemary leaves to the pan. Tip the pasta and broccoli back into the pan. Turn off the heat. Squeeze the juice of half a lemon (or more, as you like) on to the broccoli pasta.

4. Check the seasoning. Add chilli flakes, if using, and the remaining tablespoon of olive oil. Add the Parmesan and give it all a good stir to mix the broken broccoli into the pasta.

5. Serve in bowls, with extra Parmesan on top.

BAKED PASTA WITH POTATO & MOUNTAIN CHEESE

This pasta dish originates from the mountain region of northern Italy bordering Switzerland. It's traditionally made using buckwheat pasta known as pizzoccheri, dark flat freckly noodles that give flavour and ballast alongside the baked cabbage, potatoes and cheese.

A substantial wintry supper, it is best of all made with an earthy mountain-style cheese that will yield in the oven. Unbeatable with Fontina, Gruyère or even Taleggio.

I have also used flat buckwheat noodles from my local Asian grocery store if pizzoccheri have been too tricky to track down. And, at a push, for life is short and pasta shapes many, any wide flat pasta will do. Do try to use a wholewheat pasta, though, to ape the earthiness that buckwheat lends to this dish.

~ ~ ~ ~

Serves 4

- 300g (about 2 small) waxy potatoes, diced
- 40g unsalted butter
- 1 onion, finely chopped
- 2 cloves of garlic, finely chopped
- 1 small Savoy cabbage, dark outer leaves removed, inner leaves shredded
- 200g dried pasta (see above)
- 500ml béchamel sauce (see page 16)
- 80g Fontina, Gruyère or Taleggio cheese, grated
- salt and freshly ground black pepper
- a pinch of freshly grated nutmeg
- 20g Parmesan cheese, freshly grated

1. Preheat the oven to 180°C/gas mark 4.
2. Bring the potatoes to the boil in a large pan of water and cook for 15–20 minutes until just tender. Remove with a slotted spoon, drain and set aside. Keep the water on the heat.
3. While the potatoes are cooking, gently heat half the butter in a pan. Add the onion and garlic and fry for 5 minutes until soft. Remove from the pan and set aside in a large bowl.
4. Blanch the cabbage in the potato water for 30 seconds. Remove with a slotted spoon, drain and set aside.
5. Cook the pasta in the same water according to the packet instructions, until al dente. Drain, then mix with the onion, cabbage and potatoes. Transfer to a large baking dish (approx. 28 x 20cm) greased with the other half of the butter.
6. Gently reheat the béchamel sauce. Melt in the Fontina, Gruyère or Taleggio. Season with salt, pepper and nutmeg, then pour over the pasta and vegetable mix and check the seasoning.
7. Scatter the Parmesan over the top and bake for 10–15 minutes, until golden brown.

POTATO GNOCCHI

Serves 4
- 350g floury potatoes, unpeeled
- 1 egg yolk
- 50g '00' or plain flour, plus extra if needed for the dough mix and for rolling
- salt
- ¼ of a nutmeg, freshly grated

To serve
- brown butter (see page 112)
- fresh sage leaves (optional)
- tomato sauce with sage and oregano (see page 173 – optional)
- freshly grated Parmesan cheese

1. Preheat the oven to 180°C/gas mark 4.
2. Bake the potatoes for 45 minutes to an hour, until cooked through.
3. When cool enough to handle, but still warm, halve the potatoes, scoop out the flesh, and either push it through a sieve with the back of a spoon or use a potato ricer. It is important that the potato is still warm, but not too hot, when you begin to make the gnocchi dough.
4. Place the mashed potato in a large bowl. Make a well in the centre and add the egg yolk and ½–1 teaspoon of flour. Add salt and the nutmeg.
5. Using dry hands, fold the mixture together, working towards the centre. Gently knead the resulting dough, adding tiny amounts of extra flour if it is too sticky, until you have a smooth dough. But be warned: be careful not to add too much more flour than the recipe stipulates, as the more flour added the firmer the gnocchi will be.
6. Be careful not to overwork the mixture – you want to form it into a cohesive dough as quickly and with as little movement as possible. Once the gnocchi mixture has come together, rest the dough for 5 minutes.
7. Cut the gnocchi dough into four and on a very lightly floured work surface roll each piece into a long sausage shape about 2cm in diameter, then cut into 3cm lengths. Place them on a wooden board or lightly floured tray.
8. Cook the gnocchi in boiling salted water for 2–3 minutes, or until they float to the top.
9. Remove the gnocchi with a slotted spoon and put them on a warm serving plate.
10. Serve with brown butter and, if liked, some sage leaves thrown into the pan, or some tomato sauce (see page 173) with sage or oregano. Top with plenty of grated Parmesan.

Note: Once cooked these gnocchi can be stored in layers on greaseproof paper in a lightly oiled and lidded plastic tub in the fridge for up to 3 days. Stored like so, they can be fried in a non-stick pan, with a spot of olive oil, over a moderate heat until nut brown in colour. Add a knob of butter to the pan when they have taken on a nice colour. Serve as above.

SPAETZLE

Serves 4

- 200g plain flour
- salt and freshly ground black pepper
- 2 eggs
- 130ml milk
- ¼ of a nutmeg, freshly grated
- a little oil, for greasing
- 2 tbsp melted butter, to serve

1. Sift the flour into a large bowl and season with salt and pepper. Make a well in the centre of the flour, then break the eggs into this and add the milk and nutmeg. Using a wide wooden spoon or your hand like a paddle, gradually mix together, then beat the mix to try to incorporate some air into the dough.

2. Cover with clingfilm and refrigerate for an hour or so.

3. Bring a large pan of lightly salted water to the boil.

4. If you've got a potato ricer with medium-to-large holes, you can use that. Otherwise set a colander with medium-to-large holes over the pan, but do not let the water touch the bottom of the colander.

5. Taking care to avoid the hot steam, pour about a quarter of the batter into the colander and press it through the holes with a flexible spatula. Be especially careful now not to let the water touch the bottom of the colander, otherwise the holes will become blocked with semi-cooked batter.

6. The spaetzle are ready when they rise to the surface. Use a slotted spoon to fish them out and tip them on to a lightly oiled tray.

7. Continue with the remaining batter. It is best to use only a little batter at a time, because if you push too much through at once it can clump together into a large mass of spaetzle, instead of lots of little ones.

8. Toss the warm, just-boiled spaetzle in melted butter and serve as you might potatoes, rice or pasta.

VARIATION: SAUTÉD SPAETZLE WITH SHALLOTS AND ROSEMARY

This is my favourite way to eat spaetzle. Heat a large non-stick pan over a medium-high heat. Heat 1 tablespoon of unsalted butter and add 1 finely sliced shallot. Sauté for a couple of minutes, until the shallot is cooked and beginning to turn golden. Add a couple of cups of cooked (cooled is fine) spaetzle to the hot pan and let them heat for a minute in the pan before starting to toss them about. Continue to cook the spaetzle until they begin to crisp and are turning nut brown in places. Add 1 tablespoon of finely chopped fresh rosemary leaves and give the pan a good shake. Season to taste with salt and pepper and remove from the heat. Serve straight away.

COLD SICHUAN NOODLES

My Sichuanese stepmother taught me how to make these noodles. A traditional Chinese street food, they are quick to make and you can adjust the chilli blast accordingly by adding extra per bowlful for those who want it. They are my default picnic offering when weary of sandwiches and such.

~ ~ ~ ~

Serves 4

- 4 x 50–75g nests of medium wheat noodles
- 1 tbsp peanut oil or sunflower oil
- 2 tbsp Chinese sesame paste or tahini
- 1–1½ tbsp dark soy sauce
- 1–1½ tbsp light soy sauce
- 1–1½ tbsp black Chinese vinegar
- 1–1½ tbsp sesame oil
- 1 small clove of garlic, crushed and minced
- chilli oil or flakes

To serve

- a good handful of mixed sesame and sunflower seeds
- a pinch of salt
- 4 spring onions, finely sliced
- ½ a cucumber, peeled, deseeded and cut into thin strips or rounds

1. Cook the noodles according to the packet instructions. Once cooked, refresh in plenty of cold water and drain in a colander. Put them into a bowl and douse with the peanut/sunflower oil, mixing thoroughly with a couple of chopsticks to ensure they don't stick together.

2. Thin the sesame paste with about a tablespoon of water. It might look like it has split or separated, but don't worry. Once mixed with all the other sauce ingredients, the paste will amalgamate again.

3. In a bowl big enough to house your cooked noodles, mix the thinned sesame paste, soy sauces, black vinegar, sesame oil, sugar, minced garlic and chilli oil or flakes.

4. Add the cold noodles and mix thoroughly with a couple of chopsticks.

5. If the noodles seize – feel a bit too bound together – a tablespoon of cold water added to the bowl at this point will help to loosen them.

6. In a dry frying pan, toast the seeds with a pinch of salt for a few minutes until they just begin to toast, crackle and turn a golden brown.

7. To eat, divide the noodles between bowls and serve with the spring onions, cucumber and toasted seeds on top.

RICE

A grain, but deserving here of its own ballyhoo so frequently does a rice-based supper land in front of my children. Perhaps it was the trip to central China when Grace was one that sparked the rice roll. With the baby stuffed in a backpack and thinking nothing need change now we had a child (once a wanderer, always a wanderer...), it came as a surprise when she flatly refused to eat anything other than rice.

Impromptu street-food stalls, gargantuan urban restaurants and suppers with my stepmother's family... feeding our daughter on the hoof proved trickier than we had anticipated. Even when a dish of ten eggs called *jing watt dan* (which translates as 'steamed silky egg', a bit like a savoury crème brûlée) was offered by way of toddler-friendly food, the call for rice was loud and clear.

Seeing her parents eating with chopsticks, Grace's resolve to be fed likewise was steadfast. We spent a faintly ridiculous month feeding her like a baby bird: tiny clumps of rice at a time, swooped through a sauce or broth, from the end of impossibly long wooden chopsticks.

Have rice, will travel. And what a journey. First cultivated by the Chinese over 8,500 years ago, this easily grown and versatile grain is popular the world over. I've visited China, India, Thailand, Laos, Cambodia, Malaysia and Vietnam, and in those cultures rice is predominantly served plainly steamed or boiled and eaten alongside meat, fish and vegetable dishes. My children all relish a bowl of plain rice served as accompaniment. With time on my side (an extra twenty minutes should suffice), I always prefer to cook brown. I like the nuttiness and health-giving attributes of the unhusked grain.

Meanwhile, on journeys in Spain, I have loved the baked rice dishes. Paella especially is a brilliant way of cooking rice and one that makes for a convivial meal, with children and grown-ups alike delving deep to extract seafood, chicken, peppers and those golden, stuck-to-the-pan clumps of rice known as socarrat. Equally popular with my kids are the many riffs on pilaf I like to serve. Rice, lidded and cooked with stock or water, vegetables and/or meat and served with yoghurt to dollop, toasted seeds to sprinkle and lemons to squeeze. Artful is the dish of beetroot pilaf that packs a punch on the vegetable front and has your children calling for more 'pink rice'.

The process of making a risotto, among some cooks and chefs I have known, is one of great reverence. Stirring constantly, gently extracting the starch for ultimate viscosity and perfecting the 'bite' of the grain while factoring in an adequate resting time... making a good risotto is no mean feat. Give it a go.

Rice. I couldn't be without it.

KUSHARI RICE

I am ever so slightly obsessed by this Egyptian-style dish. Kushari is a brilliant way to embellish a bowl of rice. Browning the tiny pasta shapes in the foaming butter before adding the rice and lentils is essential. The toasted caramelized flavours enhance the finished dish. I also like to add a cinnamon stick or two to the pan, enjoying the perfume it releases to the grains as they cook. Topped with a straggle of softened browned onions and some tomato sauce, this is a fantastic dish for all the family. Serve on its own or as an accompaniment to fish, poultry or meat.

~ ~ ~ ~

Serves 4

- 1 tbsp butter
- 2 tbsp olive oil
- 125g little pasta shapes (such as star-shaped stelline or broken-up wheat vermicelli)
- 125g long-grain white rice, rinsed in cold water and drained
- 125g green or brown lentils, rinsed in cold water and drained
- 2 cinnamon sticks
- 1 tsp salt (optional)
- 800ml boiling water
- 4 large or 6 medium onions, sliced
- 4 tbsp spiced tomato sauce with cinnamon and allspice (see page 173)
- chilli flakes (optional)

1. Put the butter and 1 tablespoon of oil into a heavy-bottomed pan (one for which you have a tight-fitting lid) over a moderate heat. When the butter has melted, add the pasta. Stir it continuously for 5 minutes in the foaming butter and oil. You want it to colour slightly, to a nice nut brown.

2. Add the rice and lentils to the pan, then add the cinnamon sticks and salt (if using) and top with the boiling water.

3. Bring to the boil, then simmer over a low heat with the lid on.

4. Five minutes into cooking, give the pan a gentle stir to distribute the lentils, which will have risen to the top. Continue cooking with the lid firmly on.

5. After 15–20 minutes, the water should all be gone and the grains and pasta should be cooked.

6. Place a clean tea towel on top of the pan and underneath the lid – this will help draw any superfluous moisture and make the grains extra-fluffy. Leave to rest like this for 5 minutes.

7. While the rice is cooking, fry the onions in the remaining tablespoon of oil over a moderate heat. Take your time. You want the onions to melt, soften completely and gradually turn golden brown. This will take up to 20 minutes.

8. To serve, tip the kushari rice into a serving dish, spoon over some warmed sweet spiced tomato sauce and scatter over the cooked onions. Chilli flakes are nice too, for those who want them.

PINK RICE
(BEETROOT PILAF)

Note: To make brown butter, put 75g of unsalted butter into a pan over a moderate heat to melt. Once melted, the sediment (milk whey) should begin to collect and brown at the bottom of the pan. When the sediment is beginning to turn golden and brown, add the juice of half a lemon to stop the butter cooking. Unused brown butter can be kept in the fridge and warmed through when needed again.

Serves 4

For the rice

- 250g white basmati rice
- 2 tbsp olive oil
- 1 large onion, finely diced
- 3 fat cloves of garlic, finely sliced
- 2 cinnamon sticks
- 1–2 tsp each cumin, caraway and coriander seeds, ground and toasted (see page 12)
- salt
- 500g raw beetroot, grated (about 4 medium beetroot)

To serve

- a large handful of mixed sunflower and pumpkin seeds
- ½ clove of garlic, minced
- 250ml plain Greek yoghurt
- ½ a clove of garlic, minced
- 1 tbsp of extra-virgin olive oil, to top the yoghurt
- sumac, to sprinkle on the yoghurt (optional)
- 1 small bunch of chopped fresh dill, mint or coriander
- brown butter (optional)
- chilli flakes
- 1 lemon, cut into quarters, to squeeze at the table

1. Give the rice a good rinse through in a sieve under cold running cold water.

2. Put the olive oil into a heavy-bottomed medium pan (one for which you have a tight-fitting lid) over a moderate-to-low heat. Add the onion and cook gently for 10 or so minutes, until translucent and soft. Add the garlic and spices and cook for a further 3 minutes or so. Add 2 teaspoons of salt.

3. Add the washed and drained rice, then turn up the heat to moderate and move the grains around the pan to ensure they are coated with the oil, spices, onions and garlic. Toast the rice in the pan for a further minute, taking care that nothing catches and everything begins to glisten nicely.

4. Add the raw grated beetroot. Mix thoroughly.

5. Pour boiling water (from the kettle) over the beetroot and rice until the entire mix is just submerged in water. Bring to the boil, then lid the pan tightly and reduce the heat to a gentle simmer. The pilaf might benefit from a gentle turning over with a big spoon halfway through cooking, to distribute the beetroot through the rice again. Lid tightly and cook until the rice is cooked through and the liquid has gone – 15–20 minutes. Be brave: don't be tempted to add more water.

6. When the rice is cooked, put a clean tea towel under the lid, then re-seal the pan and let it rest for 5 minutes. The tea towel will remove unwanted extra moisture in the rice and make the pilaf extra-fluffy.

7. In the meantime, assemble your extras.

8. In a large dry frying pan, gently toast your seeds with a pinch of salt until they turn golden brown and begin to crackle. Put them in a bowl.

9. In a separate bowl, mix the Greek yoghurt with a pinch of salt and the garlic. Slick the top of the seasoned yoghurt with some olive oil and add a good pinch of sumac, if you have it.

10. Roughly chop your chosen herbs and put into a separate bowl.

11. Some brown butter (see note, opposite) spooned over the rice at the table is great, but optional.

12. To serve, spoon the rice on to a plate and add a blob of yoghurt, some herbs, toasted seeds, a spoonful of brown butter, if using, and a pinch of chilli flakes. Serve some lemon quarters alongside to squeeze.

SLOW-ROAST CARROTS WITH BROWN RICE

Slow-roast the carrots for about an hour – it brings out their sweetness, making them deliciously fudgy and with an intense flavour.

~ ~ ~ ~

Serves 4

For the carrots
- 1kg medium carrots, peeled and left whole, or halved lengthways if large
- 2 tbsp olive oil
- ½ a head of garlic, unpeeled and the cloves left whole
- salt and freshly ground black pepper
- 2 tbsp cumin seeds, toasted and bashed a little but not to a powder (see page 12)
- ½ a lemon (use the other ½ for the dressing below)
- 1 large bunch of fresh flat-leaf parsley, leaves finely chopped

For the fried halloumi
- 300g fresh homemade halloumi cheese (see page 23) or bought halloumi
- 1–2 tbsp olive oil

For the rice
- 250g brown rice, long-grain or short-grain as you prefer
- 1.25 litres cold water
- a pinch of salt

For the dressing
- garlic from the roasted carrots
- ½ a lemon (see above)
- 2 tbsp olive oil

1. Preheat the oven to 160°C/gas mark 3.
2. Put the carrots into a roasting tin. Add the olive oil, garlic, some salt and the toasted cumin and mix well.
3. Cover tightly with foil and roast for about 30–45 minutes, until completely tender.
4. In the meantime, cook the rice. Put the rice, water and a pinch of salt into a pan and bring it to the boil. Stir once, turn the heat to low, put a lid on the pan and simmer gently for about 40 minutes, or until the grains are tender. Drain well and keep warm.
5. When the carrots are tender, remove the foil. Take out the garlic and reserve, then put the carrots back into the oven and roast for another 15 minutes.
6. When the carrots are cooked, dress them in the roasting tin with the juice of half a lemon, the parsley and some pepper.
7. To make the dressing, squeeze out the sweet baked garlic flesh from the cloves into a bowl – it should be like a paste. Stir in the juice of the other half lemon and the olive oil.
8. Stir the dressing into the warm rice and check the seasoning.
9. To make the fried halloumi, heat a non-stick frying pan and add 1 tablespoon of the olive oil. Swirl the oil around the pan and add the halloumi in a single layer.
10. Cook for about 1 minute, then turn over and cook until golden brown on both sides. Add a little more oil if the halloumi starts to stick. Remove to a plate.
11. Spoon the rice over a big plate, add the carrots and top with the fried halloumi.

PUMPKIN, LENTIL, ALLSPICE & APRICOT PILAF

Serves 4

- 2 tbsp olive oil
- 1 large onion, diced
- 2 cloves of garlic, finely chopped
- about 500g pumpkin or squash, peeled and grated
- 200g basmati rice, soaked for 30 minutes in cold water and drained
- 100g green lentils, soaked for 30 minutes in cold water and drained
- 1½ tsp ground allspice
- 1 cinnamon stick
- 3 bay leaves
- 2 tbsp sunflower seeds, toasted (see page 64)
- 1 tsp salt
- 80g dried apricots, chopped roughly
- 700ml hot vegetable or chicken stock (see page 145) or water

To serve

- 4 tbsp brown butter (see page 112)
- 3 tbsp sunflower seeds, toasted (see page 64)
- a small bunch of fresh flat-leaf parsley, roughly chopped
- ½ tsp chilli flakes (optional)
- 250g yoghurt, seasoned with salt and pepper
- 1 lemon, cut into wedges

1. Heat the oil in a heavy-bottomed casserole over a medium heat and add the onion and garlic. Cook until soft and sweet, then add the grated pumpkin and cook for 10–15 minutes until very soft and rich, stirring and scraping regularly.

2. Add the rice, lentils, spices, bay leaves, sunflower seeds, salt and apricots. Stir well to combine, then add the hot stock or water. Bring to the boil, then reduce the heat. Put a lid on the casserole and cook for 20 or so minutes, until the lentils and rice are cooked and there is no liquid left.

3. To serve, spoon over the brown butter, sprinkle with the toasted sunflower seeds, parsley and chilli flakes, if using, and add a dollop of seasoned yoghurt. Serve with wedges of lemon.

RISOTTO

Great risotto is made when the rice is cooked with enough friction. This requires constant stirring with a wooden spoon for the grains to release their starch and make a creamy rich risotto. Toasting the rice in the softened buttery onions before you add the wine (if using) and the stock is essential. Improving the flavour, this method will also 'lock' the starch into the grain and ensure it is released gradually throughout the cooking process. After all that stirring, rest your risotto for ultimate ooze. With this basic risotto recipe mastered, add anything from peas to pumpkin and prawns via fish, chicken and vegetable stocks. Be sure you make enough to have leftovers for making arancini (see page 119).

~ ~ ~ ~

Serves 4

For the risotto base
- 1 large onion, chopped as finely as possible
- 1 tbsp butter
- 400g risotto rice (Arborio, Carnaroli or, best of all, Vialone Nano)
- 1 glass of white wine (you can just use stock from the off if you like)
- 2 litres well-flavoured hot vegetable or chicken stock (see page 145)
- salt and freshly ground black pepper

To finish
- 50g butter
- 75g Parmesan cheese, freshly grated, plus extra for sprinkling
- ½ a lemon (optional)

1. To begin your risotto, gently cook the onion in the butter over a moderate heat for at least 5 minutes until suitably soft and translucent.

2. Turn up the heat and add the risotto rice. Mix for 2 minutes or so, until the outside of the rice grain turns translucent and the rice is heated through.

3. Add the white wine, if using (you should hear your pan exhale as you do this), or a similar quantity of the stock, and mix thoroughly until the liquid has all evaporated.

4. Turn down the heat to a moderate simmer and add the hot stock, ladleful by ladleful, ensuring that each measure of liquid has evaporated before you add the next. Stir continuously. This will help in making a creamier risotto and ensure that the rice is evenly cooked.

5. Your risotto should be ready in 16–18 minutes. As you near the end of the cooking time, taste grains of rice frequently – you want the rice to be al dente. Let the risotto rest for 5 minutes off the heat with a lid on the pan.

6. To finish, vigorously beat in the 50g of butter, then the Parmesan.

7. Check for seasoning, adding salt, pepper and lemon juice as needed.

8. Serve in wide bowls or plates and sprinkle with extra Parmesan. For perfect consistency, your risotto should almost, but not quite, want to move from the one side of the plate to the other when you tip it.

ARANCINI

Any leftover risotto can also be made into these little fried rice balls, traditionally a Sicilian street food.

~ ~ ~ ~

Quantities will depend on the amount of risotto you have left over:
- leftover cold risotto (see page 116)
- tomato and herb sauce
  (see page 173)
- mozzarella cheese, cut into 1cm cubes
- plain flour, for coating
- 2 or 3 eggs, beaten
- dried breadcrumbs
- vegetable oil, for frying
- 1 lemon, cut onto wedges, to serve

1. Using wet hands, take an amount of rice about the size of a ping-pong ball in one hand and shape it into a ball. Make a deep indent with your opposite thumb to create a pocket.

2. Push a little sauce into the hole, followed by a cube of mozzarella, and close your hand tight to enclose the filling.

3. Roll the arancino in your hands to smooth the outside, then dip in the flour, then the beaten egg, then the breadcrumbs.

4. Place to one side and repeat until you have rolled all the arancini.

5. When ready to cook, heat oil to 170°C in a large saucepan (never more than one-third full) or a deep-fat fryer. A thermometer is best to check the temperature, but if you don't have one, put a cube of bread into the hot oil and it should fry golden brown in 60 seconds if the oil is hot enough.

6. In small batches, fry the arancini until golden, crisp and heated through. Drain on kitchen paper and serve with a wedge of lemon.

SPANISH BAKED RICE (ARROZ AL HORNO)

You can use boneless thighs, or chicken breast, but I prefer the extra flavour that the bones bring to the rice, as well as keeping the meat moister. There is a lot of garlic in the recipe – leave it whole in the skin so that as it cooks it sweetens and mellows. Those who find a pulpy clove of garlic on their plate to squeeze out and mash in among their rice are the lucky ones. Try to avoid any garlic that has green shoots sprouting from the middle, as the flavour will be harsher.

Saffron is expensive. Used judiciously, a little goes a long way. It is worth buying the very best quality, as the flavour is unrivalled in comparison to the cheaper stuff. Saffron flavour, colour and aroma increase with a little time spent infusing in warm water before use. Store unused saffron in a cool, dry place, away from light, and it will last very well for two years.

~ ~ ~ ~

Serves 4

- a pinch of crumbled saffron threads (optional)
- 6–8 chicken thighs (boned or whole)
- salt and freshly ground black pepper
- 1 tbsp olive oil
- 1 large onion, chopped
- 1 red pepper, deseeded and chopped
- 10 cloves of garlic, unpeeled and left whole
- 2 tsp paprika, sweet or picante (though I don't usually make this too spicy)
- 400g short-grain Spanish white rice (though you can use other short-grain varieties)
- 1 glass of white wine (optional)
- 1 litre hot chicken stock (see page 145) or boiling water
- 1 x 400g tin of plum tomatoes, drained of their juice (save this for use elsewhere)
- 2 bay leaves and a couple of sprigs of fresh thyme, tied together with string
- a small handful of fresh flat-leaf parsley, leaves chopped, to garnish

1. If using the saffron, soak it in a little warm water – about 50ml – for at least 30 minutes (though a few hours is best to extract the full flavour).

2. Preheat the oven to 180°C/gas mark 4.

3. Pat the chicken dry and season with salt and pepper. Heat the olive oil in a wide casserole over a moderately high heat until hot but not smoking, then brown the chicken on all sides, about 12 minutes in total. Transfer the chicken to a plate, leaving the cooking fat behind in the pan.

4. Add the onions and red peppers to the pot with a pinch of salt to taste. Cook over a moderate heat, stirring, until softened, about 10 minutes.

5. Add the garlic, paprika and rice, and toast and warm the rice through, stirring all the time, for about 1 minute. Return the chicken to the pot, adding any juices from the plate.

6. Add the wine (if using), or a similar quantity of stock/water, and boil uncovered for 1 minute. Then add the tomatoes, stock, bay leaves and thyme, along with the saffron and its soaking liquid.

7. Put a lid on the casserole, or cover with foil, and cook in the oven for about 30 minutes – until the chicken is cooked through, the rice is tender, and most of the liquid has been absorbed.

8. Remove from the heat and allow to rest for 5 minutes. Season with salt and pepper to taste, at the table.

PLAIN RICE

My mum taught me how to cook plain white rice. I am forever thankful, because her way is easiest and best. Whatever the quantity of rice, double it with boiling water. For example: 1 cup of rice to 2 cups of boiling water.

~ ~ ~ ~

Serves 4 as a side dish
- 1 tbsp sunflower oil
- 250g white basmati rice
- 500ml boiling water

1. Put the oil into a pan for which you have a tight-fitting lid. When hot, add the rice and give it a good stir for 30 seconds, to coat all the grains in the hot oil.

2. Add the boiling water – let the rice bubble up, then put the lid on the pan.

3. Turn down the heat to a simmer and cook for about 10–12 minutes until all the water has completely evaporated and holes/craters have appeared in the surface of the rice.

4. Remove from the heat and place a clean tea towel over the rice and under the lid. This absorbs excess moisture and makes the rice extra fluffy.

FISH

We don't cook an awful lot of fish at home. Certain species are being catastrophically over-fished. I am prudent in my use of fish and tend to rely on species that are not in a worrying state of decline.

Fish suppliers I have worked with over the past decade seem confident in the sustainability of certain fish. Depending on the method of fishing, herring, mackerel, pollock, dab, ling and anchovy are some of the more well-known species given the green flag. This seems to me to be more than enough variety to sate the appetites of diners, whether in a restaurant or at home.

As to farmed fish, the issue is a contentious one. Distressing tales of intensively reared salmon with stubby fins from net rub and flesh with a copycat chemical dye to match their wild relatives are juxtaposed with the positive aspects of mussel farming, for example. Sustainable, abundant and the least environmentally disruptive practice of all commercial fish farming, mussels are a great shellfish to cook with at home.

With scoopable shells, a perfect fit for tiny hands and the slurpable receptacle for a delicious-tasting sauce, children seem to especially relish the messy task of giving short shrift to a mountain of mussels.

Smoking your own fish is easy and a world away from those pebble-dashed vacuum packs you can buy in the supermarket. We have a smoker my mother bought us one year as a Christmas present. It wasn't terribly expensive and gives a great flavour. Alternatively, all you need is an old wok with a tight-fitting lid and a griddle that sits securely halfway within the wok.

On holiday in Cornwall, I like nothing better than to buy spanking fresh fish to cook and eat that day. Faced with a pile of mackerel, I can't help myself and will buy some to fry and some to smoke. My children love the subtle taste of home-smoked fish. The whiff of adventure that accompanies the seasoning and smoking of the fish is something they are always keen to help with.

Best-quality bought smoked fish is a fine substitute for these recipes should a mackerel haul or smoker not come your way.

SMOKING MACKEREL

Smoking fish is fun. The sweet smokiness of the flesh appeals to children. It's also a great way of preserving fresh fish to last in tip-top condition that little bit longer. If you don't own a smoker, it's easily done in a wok (see page 122).

~ ~ ~ ~

Serves 4 as a starter
- 4 medium fresh mackerel, either fillets or butterflied (opened like a book)
- 100g coarse sea salt
- 30g soft light brown sugar
- ½ tsp each fennel seeds and black peppercorns, lightly crushed
- 1 bay leaf, shredded

To finish
- freshly ground black pepper
- zest of 1 lemon, plus a few drops of lemon juice

1. Lay the fish in a non-reactive tray and carefully remove the pin-bones.

2. Scatter over all the other ingredients.

3. Cover and leave for 15–30 minutes.

4. Rinse the fish clean under a running cold tap, pat dry and lay in a single layer on the smoker rack.

5. Sprinkle the base of your hot smoker with a layer (about 5 tablespoons) of sawdust or woodchips that haven't had any chemical treatment (alternatively, you can use a mixture of 3:1 uncooked rice and dry tea-leaves mixed with 2 tablespoons of sugar).

6. Place the smoker over a high heat. As soon as the chips start to smoke, place the rack in the smoker, cover with the lid and smoke the fish until just cooked through – 6–8 minutes, depending on heat and fish size. The best way is to test a little of the flesh to see how smoked and cooked through it is.

7. Lay on a plate and coarsely grind over some black pepper and a few drops of lemon juice.

8. Serve at room temperature, with crème fraîche or soured cream flavoured with mustard and vinegar.

SMOKED MACKEREL BAKED WITH CREAM & POTATOES

Serve with a great big green salad, dressed simply and sharply with red wine vinegar and olive oil.

~ ~ ~ ~

Serves 4

- 40g unsalted butter
- 2 onions, sliced
- 300ml double cream
- 2 bay leaves
- 300ml milk
- 2 tsp Dijon mustard
- 800g waxy potatoes, peeled
  and sliced matchstick thin
- salt and freshly ground black pepper
- 4–6 smoked mackerel fillets
  (see page 124), skin and any
  pin-bones removed
- 1 tbsp breadcrumbs (optional)

1. Preheat the oven to 200°C/gas mark 6.

2. Grease an ovenproof dish with half the butter – it should be a gratin dish of a size to hold the potatoes and onions, and 5–8cm deep.

3. Put a large saucepan on a moderate heat and add the rest of the butter. Add the onions and cook until soft, translucent and just beginning to turn golden, about 10 minutes.

4. Add the cream, bay leaves, milk, mustard and potatoes, then season with salt and pepper (being careful not to over-season, as the smoked fish is salted) and cook gently until the potatoes are half cooked, about 15 minutes. Check the seasoning and remove the bay leaves.

5. Pour half the creamy potato and onion mix into the ovenproof dish, lay the smoked mackerel on top, then pour on the remaining potato and onion mix. Press down with a wooden spoon. The liquid should just cover the potatoes. If it looks a bit dry, drizzle over a bit more milk or cream.

6. Cover with foil and bake for 20 minutes, then remove the foil and turn the oven temperature down to 180°C/gas mark 4. Sprinkle lightly with the breadcrumbs, if using, and cook for another 10 minutes, until the top is golden and crisp.

SMOKED MACKEREL, BACON & GREEN BEANS

Serves 4

For the salad
- 1 small red onion, very thinly sliced
- 2 tbsp red wine vinegar
- 500g small waxy potatoes
- 300g green beans, trimmed
- 8 thin rashers of smoked streaky bacon (optional)
- 6–8 smoked mackerel fillets, skin and pin-bones removed
- 1 small bunch of fresh flat-leaf parsley, leaves roughly chopped
- salt and freshly ground black pepper

For the dressing
- 2 tsp Dijon mustard
- 1 heaped tsp capers (optional)
- 2 tbsp red wine vinegar (the vinegar that is used to soak the red onions is best)
- 6 tbsp olive oil

1. Submerge the red onions in the vinegar in a small bowl and leave to marinate for 10 minutes.
2. Cook the potatoes whole in boiling water for 15 minutes or until tender, then drain, peel and cut in half. Put aside.
3. Cook the green beans in boiling water for 5 minutes or until tender and leave to cool on a plate.
4. In a frying pan over a moderate heat, gently fry the bacon (if using) for about 10 minutes, until crisp. Cut or break into squares and put aside.
5. Tear the mackerel into large chunks.
6. Make the dressing by mixing the ingredients in a bowl or adding to a screw-top jar and shaking.
7. Put the warm cooked potatoes into a large serving bowl, spoon over the dressing, then add the drained red onions, green beans, crisp bacon (if using), mackerel and chopped parsley. Season with salt and pepper and serve.

GURKHA
MACKEREL CURRY

A Nepalese kitchen porter called Krishna, at the Gurnard's Head in Cornwall, taught me how to make this curry. In those rare moments when we all had time to sit down and eat before the start of service, this was a favourite among the staff.

The mackerel can be cooked in tranches on the bone, which will keep the fish more moist as it cooks. However, the bones can be a bit fiddly for children to tackle – so feel free to add the mackerel filleted and cut into chunks. Trout would work in lieu of mackerel.

~ ~ ~ ~

Serves 4

- 4 whole medium mackerel, cut across the bone into 5cm chunks (or 8 boned fillets cut into chunks)
- 1 tsp turmeric
- ½ tsp chilli powder
- 3 tbsp garam masala
- 1½ tsp salt
  juice of 2 lemons
- 100g plain flour
- 6 tbsp vegetable oil
- 1 tsp fenugreek seeds
- 4 medium onions, chopped
- 1 thumb-size piece of unpeeled fresh root ginger, grated
- 3 cloves of garlic, finely chopped
- 100g whole plum tomatoes, drained and chopped if tinned, peeled (see page 12), deseeded and chopped if fresh
- 2 green chillies, deseeded and chopped (optional)
- 250ml boiling water
- 1 large bunch of coriander leaves, roughly chopped

1. Put the fish into a bowl with the turmeric, chilli powder, 1 tablespoon of garam masala, ½ teaspoon of salt and the juice of 1 lemon and leave to marinate for 30 minutes.

2. Season the flour with the remaining 1 teaspoon of salt. Heat half the oil in a frying pan, then lightly coat the fish in the seasoned flour and fry until the flour coating turns crisp and golden. You don't need to cook the fish all the way through – a minute for a filleted piece of mackerel and 2 minutes for pieces on the bone. Remove and set aside.

3. Wipe out the pan and heat the remaining oil over a moderate heat. Fry the fenugreek seeds until a dark brown colour, then add the onions and cook until soft and beginning to turn golden. Add the ginger, garlic and the remaining garam masala and cook for 1–2 minutes over a slow heat.

4. Add the tomatoes and chillies (if using) and cook gently for a further 2–3 minutes.

5. Pour in the water and simmer for 10 minutes. Check the seasoning of the sauce and add the fried fish. Cook, uncovered, over a medium heat for 2–3 minutes, until the fish is cooked through.

6. Add the chopped coriander and the remaining lemon juice to the curry and serve with plain rice (see page 121).

MUSSELS WITH HARISSA & CORIANDER

Serves 4
- 75g butter, diced
- 1 small onion or 2 shallots, thinly sliced
- 1 clove of garlic, sliced
- 150ml boiling water
- 1kg fresh mussels, debearded and scrubbed
- 1–2 tbsp harissa paste (depending how hot you want the mussels to be)
- 1 small bunch of fresh coriander, leaves roughly chopped
- juice of 1 lemon or 1 orange

1. In a pot (with a tight-fitting lid) big enough to fit everything (remembering that the mussels need lots of space to expand), melt half the butter over a medium heat and cook the onion or shallots for a couple of minutes, until softened.
2. Add the garlic and cook till fragrant, about 2 minutes. Add the water and bring to a simmer.
3. Add the mussels and harissa, then cover with the lid and simmer until the mussels open (this should take about 5 minutes), shaking the pot gently a couple of times during that time. Discard any mussels that refuse to open.
4. Stir in the coriander, the rest of the butter and the citrus juice.
5. Serve with a pile of crusty bread or toast that has been rubbed with a raw clove of garlic.

~ ~ ~ ~ ~ ~ ~ ~ ~ ~ ~

RAISIN, PINE NUT & ORANGE TOPPING FOR FISH

Serves 4
- 50g raisins
- 400–600g fillets of oily or flat fish (e.g. mackerel or small plaice)
- salt
- 2 tbsp olive oil
- juice and finely grated zest of ½ a small orange
- ½ tbsp red wine vinegar
- 4 tbsp pangrattato (see page 37) or toasted breadcrumbs
- 50g pine nuts, toasted (see page 64)
- ½ tsp fennel seeds, toasted and crushed
- chilli flakes (optional)
- 1 small bunch of fresh flat-leaf parsley, leaves finely chopped

1. Preheat the oven to 200°C/gas mark 6.
2. Soak the raisins in warm water and set aside for 10 minutes. Drain then pat dry.
3. Line a baking sheet with baking parchment. Lay out the fish fillets skin side up, season with salt and drizzle with half the olive oil.
4. Whisk together the orange juice, vinegar and the rest of the olive oil and pour over the fish.
5. Mix together the breadcrumbs, soaked raisins, pine nuts, fennel seeds and orange zest, and the chilli flakes, if using. Scatter over the fish, flesh side up, and bake in the oven for 5–10 minutes until cooked. The topping should be crisp and golden.
6. Use a fish slice to transfer the fish on to plates, scooping up any stray topping. Scatter over the parsley.
7. Spoon over any remaining cooking juices and serve.

TOMATO & GINGER SAUCE

A perfect accompaniment to serve with fried or barbecued fillets of mackerel or whole sardines in the summer. The ripe tomatoes and sweet heat of ginger work particularly well with the oiliness of the fish.

~ ~ ~ ~

Serves 4

- 4 ripe red tomatoes
- 1 thumb-size piece of unpeeled fresh root ginger
- 1 tablespoon olive oil
- 1 tsp red wine vinegar
- salt and freshly ground black pepper

1. Use a box grater to grate the tomatoes into a bowl, capturing all the juice, flesh and skin.
2. Grate in the ginger and add the oil, vinegar and some salt and pepper. Taste the sauce and check you are happy with the balance.
3. Serve the sauce as is, spooned alongside barbecued or fried fillets of fish.

~ ~ ~ ~ ~ ~ ~ ~ ~ ~ ~

ANCHOVY BUTTER

Delicious. That anchovy is in the mix doesn't seem to bother my three at all. What it gives to the butter is a certain punchy resonance, sometimes called umami. I think it is unbeatable spread thickly on hot toast. Refrigerated, the butter will keep well for a week.

~ ~ ~ ~

Makes about 200g

- 150g unsalted butter
- 3 shallots
- white wine vinegar
- 1 small tin of anchovies, chopped (50g)
- ½ tsp chilli flakes
- 1 heaped tsp fresh thyme leaves

1. Cut the butter into 2.5cm cubes and set aside in a bowl to soften.
2. Dice the shallots as small as possible, then put them into a pan and just cover them with white wine vinegar.
3. Bring the shallots and vinegar to the boil and simmer vigorously for 15 minutes until all the liquid has evaporated and only the shallots remain in the pan. Spread them out on a plate to cool.
4. Add the anchovies, chilli flakes and thyme leaves, then the cooled vinegary shallots (should be about 1 heaped tablespoon).
5. Squelch the butter and other ingredients with your fingers to ensure everything is mixed together evenly.

CHICKEN
& DUCK

Where to start with chicken? Most well-thumbed, most splattered and, accordingly, one of my very favourite cookbooks is Simon Hopkinson's seminal *Roast Chicken and Other Stories* (written with Lindsey Bareham). His prose is lyrical, his recipes timeless and any bookshelves boasting a weighty cookery collection would be nothing without this book. For the definitive method on roasting chicken, Hopkinson is master.

And while we are on the subject of enlightening chicken-reading material, Hugh Fearnley-Whittingstall's writing on poultry husbandry in *The River Cottage Meat Book* is a brilliantly depressing read. A weighty text and one that, when finished, banishes any doubts you might have had about the kind of chickens we should all be purchasing.

So to my own philosophy. My children love chicken. Magnificent is the lunch where a whole roast chicken is involved. Gold-blistered skin, creamy juicy fragrant flesh, masses of vegetables, gravy, a duvet of bread sauce, the wishbone to squabble over and snap, oyster meat lurking underneath. Such a lunch is a true celebration of food and family.

As a child, shrewd to the labours of washing up, I'd always offer to dismantle the bird for my mother. Standing on a stool with a partially demolished chicken frame in front of me, there I'd stand, fingers sticky with chicken fat, prising the last bits of meat from the carcass.

The glorious thing about roasting a whole bird is the sense of continuum it gives your week's cooking. From the frame, chicken stock, simmered in water for a couple of hours with a carrot, a clove of garlic, perhaps a leek and a sprig of thyme. The chicken may be long gone, but magic is the stock that tastes of that same bird and has so many uses.

As for those salvaged morsels of meat? In summer, perhaps I'd use them with some cooked green lentils and roasted tomatoes, the beginnings of a robust salad with protein oomph. Or in winter, bathed in cream and tucked under a pie lid.

A whole bird will and should set you back a tenner. For more frugal week-night chicken requirements, I'm keen on chicken thighs. Considerably cheaper, thigh meat is flavoursome and versatile. If I am feeling especially parsimonious, I will poach the thighs in water and aromatics (as above), using the stock and meat for different dishes. You could roast the thigh meat and make a stock from the bones but the yield would be small. This way round, you've got another meal in your back pocket for later in the week and you've made an already inexpensive meat purchase stretch twice as far.

Ducks seem to have a slightly prohibitive restaurant-only reputation. A shame. With tremendous flavour and glorious fat to render the meat succulent and also to roast your spuds on a Sunday, duck is a terrific foodstuff. Your butcher may already stock duck; alternatively, you can always ask him to order you in a good-quality one.

As for chicken breasts, I can't remember the last time I bought these on their own. Expensive and the most anodyne of chicken meat as far as flavour goes. If chicken breast is your thing, far better to relish it intact and on the whole bird.

A fridge with chicken in it is a portal to great cookery. Know your way around a chicken and get busy with those thighs, wings and drumsticks. Oh! for a book with a thousand pages, for there are numerous chicken recipes worthy of note. Next time …

WHOLE CHICKEN ROASTED OVER RICE WITH CINNAMON

From my friend Jemma, whose grandmother has ultimate claim; it's been no mean feat to wrestle this recipe from her. I'll often make this for Sunday lunch with a big green salad.

~ ~ ~ ~

Serves 4
- 250g basmati rice
- 1.5kg whole chicken
- 2 tbsp (or thereabouts) olive oil
- salt and freshly ground black pepper
- 3 tsp ground cinnamon
- 1 cinnamon stick, broken in half
- 10 cardamom pods
- 2 whole allspice
- 4 bay leaves
- 2 onions, diced
- 500ml hot chicken stock
  (see page 145) or boiling water
- 1 lemon, cut into wedges to serve

1. Preheat the oven to 180°C/gas mark 4.

2. Soak the rice in a bowl of cold water while you prepare the chicken.

3. Rub the chicken with 1 tablespoon of olive oil, a heaped teaspoon of salt and half the ground cinnamon. Put half the whole spices, 2 bay leaves and an extra pinch of salt into the chicken cavity.

4. Heat a large deep heavy-bottomed casserole pan (big enough to take the whole chicken and with a tight-fitting lid – though you can use foil if necessary) over a moderate heat and pour in the remaining olive oil. Add the chicken, breast side up.

5. Put the casserole, unlidded for the time being, into the hot oven and roast for 20 minutes per 500g.

6. Meanwhile, remove the husks from the rest of the cardamoms and grind the seeds with the remaining allspice, leaving the remaining half of the cinnamon stick whole.

7. Drain the rice and take the pan from the oven and transfer the chicken to a plate. Leave the oven on.

8. Put the pan on a low heat and add the diced onions with the rest of the spices and the remaining bay leaves. Add a pinch of salt and cook the onions in the cinnamony chicken fat and olive oil, stirring often, until soft and sweet, 8–10 minutes.

9. Add the well-drained rice to the onion mix and stir well.

10. Make a well in the middle of the rice mixture and put the chicken into it. Add the hot stock or water. Bring to a simmer, then return the pan to the oven with the lid on. Cook for about 20–25 minutes, until the liquid is absorbed and the rice and chicken are cooked (the juices should run clear).

11. Remove from the oven and allow the dish to rest for 10 minutes with the lid on – I place a clean tea towel between the lid and the chicken when resting, to absorb any excess moisture in the rice.

12. Serve with wedges of lemon to squish at the table, and give the rice and chicken a final seasoning with salt and a generous grinding of pepper.

BRICK
CHICKEN

Boneless chicken thighs, squashed and cooked under a brick. The meat remains juicy and moist because it is compressed by the weight of the brick, giving it an even thickness and making the flesh cook at a uniform rate. The skin gets maximum impact from the searing heat of the pan and this makes it ridiculously crisp. My children also think cooking chicken under a brick is very amusing. You'll need a couple of clean bricks for this. Failing that, you can use a heavy ovenproof pan that will fit your frying pan. Either way, you want it to be quite heavy.

Serves 4

- marinade paste (see the 4 different marinades below)
- 8 boneless chicken thighs
- olive oil
- salt and pepper (optional)

Chilli, garlic and lemon marinade

- ½ tsp chilli flakes
- 2 cloves of garlic, crushed
- zest of 1 lemon
- 1 tsp fresh thyme leaves
- 2 tbsp olive oil

Rosemary and garlic marinade

- 2 tbsp chopped fresh rosemary leaves
- 2 cloves of garlic, crushed
- 2 tbsp olive oil

Chipotle and lime marinade

- ½ tsp chipotle chilli paste (see note)
- zest of 2 limes
- stalks from a small bunch of fresh coriander (keep the leaves for adding when chicken is cooked)
- 2 tbsp olive oil

Cumin, cardamom and cinnamon marinade

- 1 tsp each of cumin and cardamom seeds, toasted and ground (see page 12)
- 1 tsp ground cinnamon
- 2 cloves of garlic, crushed
- 1 small white onion, grated
- 2 tbsp olive oil

1. Combine the ingredients for whichever marinade you are using with a pestle and mortar or in a food processor, or just chop together with a heavy knife on a chopping board.
2. Rub the marinade all over the chicken, and put it, covered, into the fridge. For best results, marinate the chicken for at least 2 hours (overnight is best) before cooking. Alternatively, cook the chicken simply with olive oil, salt and pepper.
3. Preheat the oven to 180°C/gas mark 4.
4. When you're ready to cook, heat a heavy-bottomed ovenproof frying pan (big enough to fit the chicken in a single layer – and the bricks of course) over a high heat and add a little olive oil.
5. Season the chicken with salt and lay it in the pan skin, side down. Cover with a loose sheet of baking parchment. Place the bricks on top, pressing down so that all the chicken is in an even layer under the bricks. Fry for a minute or two over a high heat, then put the pan into the oven and cook for 8–10 minutes, or until the chicken is cooked through and the skin is super crisp.
6. When ready, let the chicken rest for 5 minutes, then slice into thick strips or keep whole if you'd rather.

Note: Don't waste the juices left in the pan – add a cautious splash (2 or 3 tablespoons) of water, stock or white wine and scrape the pan with a wooden spoon, to make a quick sauce to serve with the chicken at the table.

Chipotle chillies are smoked jalapeño peppers from Mexico. Hot, granted, but what these chillies also give is a beguiling smokiness to food. Used judiciously, I think they are a unique ingredient to use in the kitchen. You can buy chipotle chillies dried and rehydrate them in water to pound to a paste, or buy them already processed and by the tin.

CHICKEN SHAWARMA WITH CHOP-CHOP & HUMMUS

Sandwiches made mighty. Much as I'd love one, we don't have a vertical spit at home to slow-roast meat kebab-style. A correctly prepared spit-roast shawarma is a triumph. The term can also refer to the preparation of the pitta, sandwich or wrap into which cooked sliced meat is placed, making this an easy dish to create at home.

The turmeric yoghurt marinade for the chicken tenderizes the meat and gives the cooked chicken a lovely yellow glow. Sliced warm into strips and heaped into a pitta with a good slathering of hummus, you have the beginnings of a great sandwich. Chop-chop salad is a terrific addition. Simply, favourite salad items cut up small: cucumber, tomato, spring onion and coriander leaf chopped with the juice of half a lime would be my suggestion.

~ ~ ~ ~

Serves 4

- 6 boneless chicken thighs (or ask your butcher to take the bones out)
- 4 tbsp plain yoghurt
- 1 tsp turmeric
- 1 thumb-size piece of unpeeled fresh root ginger, grated
- 4 cloves of garlic, unpeeled, bashed with the back of a knife
- 1 small bunch of fresh coriander, separated into stalks and leaves
- 1 tsp salt
- 4 pitta breads or flatbreads, plus extra to serve (see page 32)
- 1 cucumber
- 4 tomatoes
- 1 lemon
- 1 quantity hummus (see page 86)

1. Half a day before you want to cook, marinate the chicken thighs in a bowl with the yoghurt, turmeric, ginger, garlic and the stalks of the coriander.

2. Preheat the oven to 180°C/gas mark 4. Sprinkle the chicken with the salt and spread in an even layer on a baking tray. Put into the oven and bake for 40–50 minutes, until cooked through. Leave to cool slightly while you prepare the salad.

3. Chop the cucumber and tomatoes into small dice and put into a bowl with the coriander leaves and lemon juice to taste.

4. Toast the pitta bread, then slice open at one end and push some hummus in with a knife.

5. Holding the pitta beneath like a cup/pocket, insert the warm sliced chicken and sprinkle with the chop-chop. Use any extra flatbreads to mop up the yoghurty chicken juices.

WHOLE POACHED CHICKEN WITH AÏOLI

A different take on to roast chicken. With all the same majesty a whole bird presents, but here the chicken is pot-roasted and bathed in the very best sort of broth. If the method of bringing to the boil, then cooling completely the as yet not fully cooked chicken in the broth before bringing it to the boil and simmering to finish seems unusual, I can only assure you that this method makes for the most succulent chicken meat. Ever.

A Chinese technique to poaching whole chickens, which ensures the meat remains moist and full of flavour. I must also credit Fergus Henderson of St John restaurant in London for this take on poaching chickens.

~ ~ ~ ~

Serves 4, with leftovers

- 1.5kg whole chicken or 6 chicken legs
- 2 carrots, chopped
- 1 onion, halved
- 2 cloves of garlic, unpeeled and bashed with the side of a heavy knife
- 2 celery sticks, chopped
- 2 sprigs of fresh thyme
- 2 bay leaves
- 2 sprigs of fresh parsley
- 1 generous tsp whole black peppercorns
- coarse sea salt and freshly ground black pepper
- 2 leeks, washed and cut into 1cm slices
- 1 quantity of aïoli, to serve (see page 53)

1. If using a whole chicken, slit the skin between the leg and the breast, making the legs a little more slack and allowing for the liquid to circulate more freely during the cooking time.

2. Place the chicken and all the rest of the ingredients, except the leeks, in a large pan, cover with cold water and bring to the boil. As soon as it boils, cover the pan with a lid, take it off the heat and leave to cool completely. This can take upwards of 6 hours. The cooling process is important and makes the chicken meat extremely moist. By all means leave the pot in the fridge overnight ready to cook through the next day.

3. When ready to eat, transfer the chicken, whole and intact, to a waiting plate. Strain the stock. Clean out the pan and pour the stock back in. Return the chicken to the pan. Bring the chicken and broth to a gentle simmer over a moderate heat, then reduce the heat and simmer gently for 30 minutes.

4. Meanwhile, remove a little of the stock and pour just enough into a separate pan to cook the leeks for 5–7 minutes at a gentle simmer until tender. Add the cooked leeks to the pan with the chicken and broth when ready to serve. Cooking the leeks with the chicken will overpower the broth. Far better to cook them separately and introduce them when ready to serve.

5. Carve the chicken and serve with the leeks, a little of the hot broth and a bowl of aïoli to dollop at the table.

Note: Any excess broth can be frozen and used as stock.

CHICKEN STOCK

I'm sure you know, but just in case. Ask your butcher for any spare chicken bones, or use the frame and carcass scrapes from a whole cooked bird. You can make stock from smaller quantities of meat – just remember that the ratio of water is always about double that of bones (e.g. 500g bones = 1 litre water).

~ ~ ~ ~

Makes about 3 litres

- 1.5kg chicken bones (carcasses or wings) or leftover chicken scraps
- 2 onions, roughly chopped
- 1 celery stick
- 1 carrot, peeled
- 10 black peppercorns
- 2 bay leaves
- 1 small sprig of fresh thyme
- a few fresh parsley stalks

1. If using fresh chicken bones, wash them in cold water to remove any blood.
2. Place in a large pan with the onions and vegetables and add cold water until the chicken is just covered (about 3 litres).
3. Put over a high heat and bring to the boil.
4. As the stock comes to the boil, froth will appear on the surface. Skim this off and discard.
5. As soon as the stock comes to the boil, turn down the heat and allow it to simmer very gently for 3–4 hours, skimming as necessary and topping up with a little bit of cold water if the bones aren't submerged.
6. Pass through a fine sieve and allow to cool before refrigerating or freezing.
7. The stock will keep for about 4 days in the fridge or 2–3 months in the freezer.

SWEET & SOUR CHICKEN WINGS

Elbows on the table are to be encouraged here. A plate of wings, piled high and teetering, a mish-mash of chicken limbs, makes their demolition a pleasantly messy task.

Baked not fried. Spiced and sticky with tamarind and fiery gingery juices, these wings aren't artificially bloated and coated with flour or a batter. Sweet, sour and rich, tamarind is a terrific ingredient to store in your fridge. I buy mine in a block at my local Indian supermarket. Refrigerated, it will keep well for months. Use it in marinades, or stirred through a dhal towards the end of cooking for fruity tartness. I also quite like a spoonful of the pulp (perhaps a pinch of sugar too) in a tall glass with ice and topped up with soda for a refreshing fizzy drink.

For the best flavour, buy the tamarind block whole with the seeds and skin intact. To extract the smooth purée, simply put the required amount into enough warm water to just cover it and leave to soak for 15 minutes. Then squash and squeeze the softened fruit with your hands or the back of a spoon, pushing the smooth pulp through a sieve. Discard the seeds and other fibres.

~ ~ ~ ~

Serves 4
- 12 big chicken wings
- salt

For the marinade
- 120g sieved tamarind pulp (see above)
- 4 tbsp soft light brown sugar
- 2 tbsp fish sauce
- 2 cloves of garlic, crushed
- 1 thumb-size piece of unpeeled root ginger, grated
- 1 tsp chilli flakes
- 3 tbsp vegetable oil

1. Combine all the marinade ingredients in a large bowl.
2. Add the chicken wings, coating them in the marinade. Marinate in the fridge or for at least several hours, and up to 2 days.
3. When you're ready to cook, preheat the oven to 200°C/gas mark 6.
4. Arrange the wings on a baking sheet lined with baking parchment (much easier to clean up), brush with the marinade and sprinkle with a touch of salt.
5. Bake for 25–30 minutes, until the wings are nicely browned and caramelized.
6. Serve with plenty of paper napkins!

CONFIT
DUCK LEGS

Duck slow-cooked in duck fat is meltingly tender and an age-old method of meat preservation. It is also considered to be a bit of a restauranty, hell's bells, even a cheffy dish. This is such a shame, as it's easy to make and an incredibly versatile and failsafe ingredient to have to hand in your fridge. For the initial confit you'll need to buy some extra duck fat – this can be used many times over for further confit and for any other roasting and frying that will benefit from this tasty cooking fat.

~ ~ ~ ~

Serves 4
- 4 duck legs
- 800g duck fat

For the marinade
- 30g coarse sea or rock salt
- 10g soft light brown sugar
- 1 tsp black peppercorns, crushed
- 4 cloves of garlic, sliced
- 2 bay leaves, thinly sliced
- 1 tbsp fresh thyme leaves
- ½ tsp Chinese five-spice
- zest of 1 orange

1. Lay the duck legs on a tray, flesh side upwards, and scatter all the marinade ingredients evenly over, rubbing them in lightly as you go. Cover with clingfilm and leave to marinate for 12 hours or overnight.

2. Wash off the marinade and pat very dry with kitchen paper.

3. Gently melt the duck fat in a pan wide enough to contain the legs in a snug single layer if possible, then put the duck legs in skin side down.

4. Bring the temperature to 85–90°C. Use a meat thermometer to check. At this temperature there should be no bubbles breaking the surface, as the fat is kept just under simmering point.

5. Cook for 2–3 hours, or until the meat is very tender.

6. With a slotted spoon, lift the legs out of the duck fat and put to one side, reserving the melted fat.

7. If you want to store the duck confit (it will last for many months), place the legs, drained of any meaty juice, in a container and pour over the warmed duck fat. Make sure the legs are completely submerged in the fat and store, covered, in the fridge.

SALAD OF CRISP DUCK, PICKLED CARROT & MINT

A grown-up-sounding salad this may be, but I've found its appeal to be universal … there's certainly never any left when I serve it at home.

~ ~ ~ ~

Serves 4

For the pickled carrots
- 150ml cold water
- 130ml cider vinegar
- 25g caster sugar
- 1 clove of garlic, lightly crushed
- 1½ tsp caraway or fennel seeds
- 1½ tbsp coarse sea salt
- 1 bay leaf
- 200g medium carrots, peeled and halved lengthways

To assemble the salad
- 4 confit duck legs (see page 147)
- freshly ground black pepper
- 1 bunch of spring onions, sliced
- 1 small bunch of fresh mint, leaves picked
- 2 tbsp melted duck fat

1. To make the pickled carrots, put all the ingredients apart from the carrots into a non-reactive pan and bring to the boil. Remove from the heat and allow to cool completely.

2. Bring a large pan of water to the boil and blanch the carrots for 1 minute only. Drain, then cool them down under cold running water. Drain again.

3. Add the carrots to the cooled pickling liquid and leave for at least 24 hours before eating. They will keep well in the fridge for a month or so.

4. To assemble the salad, pull or cut the duck off the bone into biggish chunks, taking care to keep the skin intact, and season with a good grinding of black pepper.

5. Cut the pickled carrots into 1cm-thick slices and place in a serving bowl with the spring onions and mint leaves.

6. Heat the duck fat in a frying pan over a moderate heat and add the duck, skin side down where applicable. Brown the meat for 3–4 minutes, until crisp and heated through.

7. Transfer the cooked duck to the bowl and toss with the carrots, spring onions and mint. Use a little of the pickling liquid to dress the salad, adding extra punch and acidity.

CRISP DUCK, HOISIN, CUCUMBER & SPRING ONION

We ate this simple dish while staying high up in a mountain lodge near the city of Chengdu, on a trip to China with our daughter Grace. There the hoisin was served as a dipping sauce, all tantalizingly spicy-sweet alongside the crisp duck, vegetables and ever-present steaming bowls of plain boiled rice.

Serve Chinese-style, as one dish among others to share at the table.

~ ~ ~ ~

Serves 4
- 4 confit duck legs (see page 147)
- ½ tsp Chinese five-spice
- 1 tbsp duck fat
- 1 cucumber, halved, seeds removed, cut at an angle into half-moons
- 1 bunch of spring onions, cut into matchsticks
- 10 or so radishes, cut in half (optional)
- hoisin sauce (enough to dip, as you like)

1. Pull or cut the duck off the bone in chunks, taking care to keep the skin intact, and toss the pieces in the five-spice.
2. Heat the duck fat in a frying pan over a high heat and add the duck, skin side down where applicable. Turn the heat down and brown for 3–4 minutes, until crisp and heated through.
3. Serve the hot duck with the cucumber pieces, spring onions and radishes, if using, with a bowl of hoisin sauce to dip.

MEAT

I like going to the butcher's. I love the cool tiled walls, the soft groove of the butcher's block worn by years of chopping, the striped aprons, the pork pie hats, even the wink and a nod (all butchers I have known are masters at this) – but most of all, I like it that the meat isn't suffocated in tight cellophane.

Meat bought from a butcher's shop has a lineage. It feels like you are purchasing meat from an animal. Those squeaky clean and bloodless plastic containers on the chilly meat aisle in the supermarket feel remote, almost alien, from the field and slaughterhouse.

Family folklore has it that I cut my first tooth on a shard of biltong. Salted and spiced, chewing these blackened strips of beef leather instantly transports me back to my barefoot childhood, with the red dust of Africa chalking my toes.

Though I love eating and cooking meat, we don't eat it all that often in our house. I'd rather pay more for meat and eat less of it than eat an intensively farmed pig reared at breakneck speed. Getting to know your butcher is paramount in the grand scheme of family cooking. A good butcher should encourage you to experiment with different cuts and in doing so you will be a more imaginative cook and, ultimately, a more resourceful carnivore.

Wintry Sundays might see me splash out on a whole joint of meat to roast in the oven for family and friends. But for the mainstay I have learnt to navigate that meaty cabinet and seek out the cheaper, more thrifty cuts of meat to use in my cooking. Oxtail, mince, ham hocks and shoulder of lamb all find space on my stove top.

MEATLOAF

Due for a revival, make this and you and yours will be cock-a-hoop.

~ ~ ~ ~

Serves 4

- 2 medium onions, finely chopped
- 2 tbsp vegetable oil or equivalent of butter
- 1 large carrot, peeled and grated
- 750g minced beef
- 2 eggs, beaten
- 1 clove of garlic, crushed
- 2 tbsp finely chopped fresh flat-leaf parsley
- 1 tbsp finely chopped fresh rosemary leaves
- 3 bay leaves
- 1 tbsp mustard (I like Dijon)
- 1 tbsp Worcestershire sauce
- 50g fresh breadcrumbs
- 10g Parmesan cheese, freshly grated
- salt and freshly ground black pepper
- 150ml cold chicken, ham (see pages 145 and 165) or beef stock, or water

1. Preheat the oven to 180°C/gas mark 4.

2. Cook the onions in a little oil or butter in a pan until soft but not coloured – about 5 minutes. Add the carrot and cook for another 2 minutes, then remove to a plate and leave to cool.

3. Place all the ingredients, including the cooled vegetables and the stock, in a large mixing bowl and mix thoroughly – it is best to use your hands here.

4. Transfer the mix to a 900g loaf tin lined along the bottom with baking parchment (leave some poking out at either end to make it easier to remove from the tin). Pat down until level. Cover the top of the mixture with another piece of greaseproof.

5. Bake in the oven for 1 hour cover 15 minutes, until the meatloaf is cooked through. (Remove the paper cover 15 minutes before the end of cooking to allow the top to colour nicely.)

6. Rest for 10 minutes before cutting.

7. Best served with some warmed tomato sauce (see pages 172–173), new potatoes and a great big green salad, or with some swede and carrot mash (see page 190).

MEATBALLS

I use an egg and some stale white breadcrumbs to bind the mince in these meatballs. To my mind, meatballs merit from this addition to soften and break up the meaty mass. It also stretches the quantity of mince quite considerably. Best served with large, robust pasta like Rigatoni or large Conchiglie.

~ ~ ~ ~

Serves 4

- 65g fine dried white breadcrumbs
- 80ml milk
- 300g minced beef
- 300g minced pork
- 1 dsp fresh thyme leaves
- 1 tsp ground allspice (whole berries freshly ground is best)
- 1 egg
- salt and freshly ground black pepper
- vegetable oil, for frying
- 1 recipe of tomato and herb sauce (see page 173)

1. Put the breadcrumbs into a bowl with the milk and leave to soak for 10 or so minutes.

2. Put both the minces into a separate bowl with the thyme, allspice, unbeaten egg, salt (about half a teaspoon, but as you wish) and freshly ground pepper.

3. Add the soaked breadcrumbs to the mince mix and give the whole thing a good squishing and squeezing to combine. I like to almost knead the mix in the bowl for a couple of minutes, to tenderize and amalgamate the meat.

4. Wet your hands and roll the mince into little balls each about the size of a ping-pong ball. Put the balls on a plate in the fridge for 30 minutes to firm up.

5. Heat the vegetable oil in a frying pan over a high heat and brown the meatballs in batches. There is no need to cook them all the way through. Meanwhile, in a heavy-bottomed casserole, heat enough tomato sauce to serve with the meatballs.

6. As the balls are browned, add them to the hot tomato sauce. When they are all in, bring to a steady simmer, then turn down to a low simmer, put a lid on the pan, and continue cooking for 40 minutes.

LAMB & QUINCE TAGINE

I don't brown my meat in a tagine as it would burn the spices – more important, I think, is to give the meat and spices plenty of time to marinate before cooking. This might seem a long recipe, but it really is very easy. When quinces are out of season, replace them here with fresh or dried apricots.

~ ~ ~ ~

Serves 4

For the meat
- ½ tsp cumin seeds
- ½ tsp coriander seeds
- a pinch of chilli flakes
- 1½ tsp ground ginger
- 1 cinnamon stick
- 1kg lamb or mutton shoulder, meat diced and without too much fat (ask your butcher)
- salt
- 2 plum tomatoes peeled (see page 12) or tinned and crushed
- 2 medium onions, diced
- 3 cloves of garlic, finely chopped
- 30g butter
- 300ml chicken stock or water
- ¼ tsp saffron threads, crushed and soaked in 2 tbsp hot water for at least 20 minutes
- 1 large bunch of fresh coriander, leaves coarsely chopped, stalks reserved and chopped

For the quinces
- 2 tbsp caster sugar
- 2 medium quinces (about 200g each)
- 6 tbsp raisins
- 1 tbsp butter
- ½ tsp ground cinnamon

1. Toast the cumin and coriander seeds in a dry pan until aromatic and grind together, then mix with the other dried spices.

2. In a large bowl, mix together the meat, teaspoon of salt, the tomatoes, onions, garlic and dried spice mix. Cover and refrigerate for a couple of hours – overnight is best.

3. Put the marinated meat into a large heavy-bottomed pan, add the butter and cook over a moderate heat, uncovered, for 20 minutes, stirring occasionally.

4. After that time, add the stock or water, along with the saffron and the coriander stalks. Stir well, then cover with a lid and simmer gently over a low heat for about 2 hours, or until the meat is meltingly tender.

5. Meanwhile, cook the quinces. Bring a small saucepan of water to the boil with the sugar. Peel, core and quarter the quinces and drop into the water. Bring back to the boil, then reduce the heat and poach until tender but still holding their shape.

6. Lift out the quince pieces with a slotted spoon and set aside, keeping the cooking liquid. Pour some of the quince water over the raisins and leave to soak until plumped.

7. To finish the lamb, remove the meat from the sauce and keep nearby on a warm plate. Skim any excess fat from the sauce using a ladle. If the sauce needs thickening slightly, boil rapidly, uncovered, for a short time. Add some of the quince liquid, to taste. You want the sauce to be a balance of meat, spice and fruit flavours. Season with salt as necessary. Return the meat to the sauce and keep warm, ready to serve.

8. To finish the quinces: drain the raisins, then heat the additional butter over a moderate heat in a frying pan, preferably non-stick. Add the quinces and cinnamon and fry for 3 minutes on each side until golden and glazed all over. Then add the raisins and toss gently together.

9. To serve, arrange the quinces and raisins over the tagine meat in a warm serving dish and scatter over the coriander leaves.

LAHMACUN

Ahhh, Turkish lahmacun (pronounced lah-ma-jun). Like pizza, but topped with spiced fried lamb mince, rolled up and eaten with lots of fresh flat-leaf parsley, ripe tomatoes and squirted with lemon. We've eaten vast piles of lahmacun on holidays in northern Cyprus and I've also had some very good ones from restaurants in the Turkish community of north London. Thankfully, they are also pretty easy to make at home. Hot pepper paste is available from good Turkish grocers and will keep very well for months in the fridge. If you can't get hold of any, you can replace it with some tomato paste spiked with a bit of chilli.

I like to cook lahmacun (and pizza) on a pizza stone. Blasted in a hot oven on maximum heat, these ceramic stones can ape a commercial pizza oven for cooking a perfect crisp base. They're not expensive. A flat oven tray or baking sheet will work, but is not ideal, as these don't get as hot and do tend to warp, making the dough base cook unevenly. In winter, I might replace the tomato with a drizzle of pomegranate molasses, some toasted pine nuts but stick with the parsley.

~ ~ ~ ~

Serves 4

- plain flour, for dusting
- 1 recipe basic bread dough (see page 30) cut into 8 pieces at step 6 of the method

For the topping

- 1 medium onion, chopped
- 2 plum tomatoes, peeled (see page 12) and deseeded, or tinned
- 1 small green/red pepper, deseeded and chopped very finely
- 1 tbsp olive oil
- 1 tsp hot pepper paste
- ½ tsp caraway seeds, toasted and ground (see page 12)
- a pinch of ground cinnamon
- ½ tsp salt
- 200g minced lamb

To serve

- 1 lemon, cut into wedges
- 1 large bunch of fresh flat-leaf parsley, roughly chopped
- ripe tomatoes (if in season), sliced

1. Preheat the oven to maximum – 240°C+/gas mark 9 – and put a pizza stone or baking tray in to heat up.
2. Put the onion, plum tomatoes, pepper, olive oil, pepper paste, spices and salt into a food processor or blender and pulse until you have a coarse paste. Do not over-mix.
3. Pour into a bowl and mix in the minced lamb thoroughly, using your hands. Set aside.
4. On a well-floured work surface, roll and stretch each dough ball into a thin oval (the traditional shape) or whatever shape is easiest for you. You want to get the dough as thin as possible without tearing or making any holes.
5. Carefully remove the pizza stone or baking tray from the oven and place on a heatproof surface.
6. Lay the lahmacun on the tray and use a spoon to smear a thin layer of the topping all over the dough – taking care to not tear the base.
7. Bake for 6–8 minutes, until the dough is crisp and the topping is well cooked. Serve immediately, with lemon wedges, parsley and sliced tomatoes (if using).

PORK COOKED IN MILK

Hands down an ugly-beautiful dish. The milk will separate (curdle) with the lemon during the cooking process. Cooked in the milk whey, the meat remains moist and is surrounded by a rich and delicious juice with fabulous porky cinnamon and sage curds to spoon over.

~ ~ ~ ~

Serves 4, with leftovers (maybe)

- 2 tbsp olive oil
- salt and freshly ground black pepper
- 1.5kg boned and rolled pork collar
- 50g butter
- 6–8 cloves of garlic, peeled but kept whole (remove any green shoots in the middle by cutting in half and taking out)
- 10 fresh sage leaves
- peel (scraped of its white pith) of 1 lemon (preferably unwaxed)
- ¼ of a nutmeg, freshly grated
- 1 grated cinnamon stick
- 1 litre full-fat milk

1. Preheat the oven to 180°C/gas mark 4.
2. Use a large, heavy-based, lidded casserole which will snugly hold the pork in one piece. Place it over a medium heat and add the oil.
3. Salt the pork and brown it all over in the casserole, adding the butter towards the end of the browning process. Don't let the butter burn. Turn off the heat when the butter is brown and beginning to foam (if the butter does catch, or if the oil and butter have grown too dark, remove the pork to a plate and wipe out the pan).
4. Return the pan to the heat and return the pork to the pan. Add the garlic, sage, lemon peel, nutmeg and cinnamon stick and pour over the milk. Season with salt and pepper. Heat until the milk is just beginning to simmer, then remove from the heat.
5. Cut a piece of baking parchment that fits the casserole (a good trick is to wet it, scrunch it up, then cover the dish – you'll find the paper will then cling and cover more effectively).
6. Place the lid on the pan and put it into the oven to cook for 1½–2 hours, until the pork is cooked, tender and succulent. A knife should pierce the meat easily. The milk should have separated into lightly caramelized milk curds and have a rich clear pork whey stock.
7. Remove the lemon peel, cinnamon stick and sage leaves and mash the softened garlic cloves into the milk stock as you find them.
8. Check the seasoning, perhaps adding more freshly ground black pepper, then slice the pork and spoon over the curds and juices.

Note: This is also delicious eaten cold, and any leftovers can be reheated and broken down a little, together with a spoon or so of crème fraîche, to make an excellent pasta sauce to serve with grated Parmesan sprinkled over.

Ham hock, also known as pig's knuckle, is the ankle meat beneath the leg and before the foot and trotter. Ask your butcher for a ham hock and you'll be amazed at how little it costs. Cooked long and slow with a few friendly additions to the pot, a hock should give you plenty of meat for one meal and a good quantity of stock for a soup or braise. Hock meat is incredibly flavoursome. The knuckle is surrounded with fat and collagen. This breaks down during the cooking process, making the meat especially soft and melting.

Ham hocks are brined and sold in vacuum packs by all good butchers. I like to cook with a smoked hock rather than a green (unsmoked) hock, as it's more flavourful and I thrive on how many meals I can make from the one hock. Shred the meat for choucroute, barley broth, a mighty doorstop sandwich or to use in a salad with a mustardy dressing, some watercress and lentils.

Whether smoked or green, cover the hock with plenty of cold water and leave to soak overnight – this will temper the salt levels caused by the brining process. Throwing the water away and refreshing it a few times will also be of benefit. If cooking the hock on the day, put it into a large saucepan, cover with cold water and bring to the boil. Drain the hock and discard the water.

With the hock desalinated, put it into a large saucepan and cover it with fresh cold water. Add 1 halved onion, 2 halved celery sticks, 10 peppercorns, 2 bay leaves, a large sprig of fresh thyme, 6 fresh parsley stalks, 10 or so fennel seeds and a bashed clove of garlic with the skin still on. If you only have an onion and a bay leaf or some thyme and the celery, worry not – no one thing is crucial, except the water. Bring to the boil and skim off any frothy foamy stuff. Taste the stock for saltiness – if still too salty, repeat the process by bringing to the boil and discarding the water once again. Reduce the heat, then partially cover the pot with a lid and cook at a simmer for about 3 hours. When cooked, the meat should easily pull away from the bone with a skewer or fork. Leave the hock to cool in the liquid.

Remove the hock from the stock and shred the meat for use or leave whole to roast as a joint. Strain the stock and refrigerate or freeze to use accordingly. Freezing the stock in ice cube trays will give you ever-handy blocks of stock to use in your cooking. Once cooked, the hock will keep for a good few days in the fridge.

VARIATION: ROASTED HAM HOCK

A thrifty and impressive alternative to the roasted Sunday joint of meat. First prepare as above. Preheat the oven to 180°C/gas mark 4. Mix together 4 tablespoons of honey, 2 tablespoons of grain mustard, 4 tablespoons of fruit juice (orange, apple or pineapple) and 1 tablespoon of soft dark brown sugar. Smear this mixture all over the cooked meat, then stud the hock with 10 cloves. Put the hock into a roasting tin lined with baking parchment. Bake in the oven for about 45 minutes, basting every 10 or so minutes, until nicely coloured and glazed. Serve hot or cold – the hock is especially nice with slaw (see page 206).

SAUSAGE ROLLS

Adding stock or water to the mince will make the sausage in your roll all the more succulent and juicy.

~ ~ ~ ~

Makes 4–6 sausage rolls, depending how big you want them

For the pastry

- 350g all-butter shop-bought puff pastry, or use the cheat puff pastry below

For the filling

- 650g minced pork
- 200g pork fat, minced (ask your butcher)
- 100g fresh breadcrumbs
- 100ml cold pork or chicken stock (see page 145), or water
- 2 tsp finely chopped fresh sage leaves
- sea salt and freshly ground black pepper

To finish

- 1 egg, beaten
- poppy seeds (optional)

1. Put all the filling ingredients into a large bowl and mix until well combined. Keep in the fridge until ready to use.
2. When ready to make the rolls, preheat the oven to 180°C/gas mark 4 and line a baking tray with baking parchment.
3. Roll the pastry out to a rectangle approximately 40 x 25cm.
4. Shape the filling into a long sausage shape along the length to one side of the pastry of the pastry.
5. Brush the unfilled part of the pastry with beaten egg, then roll over and crimp the join together.
6. Cut into sausage rolls (each about 10cm long).
7. Brush the outside of the rolls with egg, sprinkle with poppy seeds, if using, then place on the baking tray and cook for 40–50 minutes.
8. Allow to rest for 10 minutes before serving, if you can resist.

~ ~ ~ ~

Puff pastry (cheat method)

1. Grate 175g of very cold butter into 225g of plain flour.
2. Stir with a knife until all the butter is well coated.
3. Pour in just enough iced water to bring it all together into a dough.
4. Roll into a ball and put into the fridge, well wrapped, to chill for an hour.
5. Roll out as per method above.

SICHUAN OXTAIL STEW

Sichuan because of the peppercorns. Sichuan peppercorns are not hot or spicy but give an intriguing buzz to cooking. While not essential in this recipe, the peppercorns are worth seeking out to experiment with. My children really enjoy the tingly sensation they emit. The triumvirate of Sichuan peppercorns, ginger and star anise is specific to Sichuan cuisine. Serve the oxtail stew with plain rice and top with sliced spring onions and some toasted sesame seeds. And mention the cow tail at your peril.

~ ~ ~ ~

Serves 4

- 1 tbsp plain flour
- salt and freshly ground black pepper
- 1kg oxtail, cut into pieces (your butcher will do this)
- 2 tbsp vegetable oil
- 5 cloves of garlic, peeled and left whole
- 5cm piece of unpeeled fresh root ginger, sliced into 6 8 pieces
- 1 tsp Sichuan peppercorns
- 1 cinnamon stick
- 4 whole star anise
- 4 strips of orange peel, pith removed
- 4 bay leaves
- 2 tbsp dark soy sauce
- 4 large carrots, peeled and chopped into 5cm lengths
- 1 glass of red wine (optional)

To serve

- 4 spring onions, finely sliced
- 1 tbsp sesame seeds, toasted (see page 12)
- chilli oil (I buy mine ready made from a Chinese supermarket, but my stepmother would always make her own with hot chilli flakes, some fierce heat and sunflower oil)

1. Put the flour into a used but clean plastic bag and add a good pinch of salt and the oxtail pieces. Hold the bag tight shut and give it a good shaking to coat the oxtail.

2. In a heavy-bottomed casserole pan into which the oxtail will fit in a single layer, heat the oil. When hot, add the floured oxtail pieces in batches and brown all over. Remove and put them on a plate as you continue with the rest.

3. Give the pan a good wipe, to get rid of any burnt oily flour residue. Put the browned oxtail pieces back into the pan.

4. Add all the other ingredients, including the wine if using, and top up with cold water. You want the oxtail to be just submerged. Don't add salt, as the soy sauce is salty and you can adjust the seasoning at the end of the cooking time.

5. Bring to the boil, then turn down the heat to a simmer, skimming off and discarding any froth that appears on top.

6. Lid the pan, leaving a slight gap, and simmer for at least 3 hours, stirring occasionally and adding water as needed to keep the oxtail submerged.

7. At the end of the simmering time, the oxtail pieces should be very tender and the meat will pull away from the bone but not completely separate from it.

8. Remove the oxtail pieces to a plate. Drain the broth through a sieve, discarding the spices, peel, bay leaves and ginger, and return the broth, including the garlic and carrots, to the pot.

9. Taste the broth for salt and return the oxtail pieces to the pan. (Optional: if you want, you can shred the meat from the bones before returning it to the broth.)

10. Serve with plain boiled rice (see page 121) and topped with sliced spring onions, toasted sesame seeds and chilli oil for those wanting extra spice.

FRUIT VEGETABLES

It's the trick question used to fox the young tomato hater: 'Fruit or vegetable?' Drum roll ... 'Ah-ha, it's a fruit!' With tomatoes then golloped back greedily and for ever more (supposedly).

Not so my children and many others. Fresh tomatoes (like courgettes and peppers, a fruit because they contain seeds) are for the most part hugely disappointing. Pity the poor supermarket tomato, sliced raw for a salad in deepest winter. Pity more the person eating it. With the exception of tomatoes grown in hot summer sunshine and left on the vine to ripen, I always prefer to use good-quality tinned ones in my cooking.

Ever popular and a stalwart of the store cupboard, tinned tomatoes are a widespread ingredient in many soups, stews, sauces and braised dishes. They can, however, bring a certain homogeneity to home cooking if the whole tin is upended into a pan. A far better, more thoughtful and thrifty way to use tinned tomatoes is to think of the contents as two different tomato ingredients, with very different uses.

Use the whole tomatoes in your cooking as you would a fresh ripe tomato, or in recipes that call for peeled. Give the tomato a gentle squeeze to extract any the watery juice and seeds. Used like so, whole tomatoes roasted, for example, with squash or pumpkin, cloves of garlic, olive oil and rosemary will make for a tray of sweetly fragrant juicy vegetables.

Drain the juice from the tin and reserve it in the fridge to use as and when to impart tomato flavour. This rich tomato juice is especially useful in soups and sauces or in recipes that call for passata. Add just enough to a Bolognese sauce and it should bring enough tang and acidity to flatter the fattiness of the meat and not detract from what should be an intensely meaty and savoury sauce. Adding the contents of a whole tin – tomatoes and juice – I think is unnecessary and makes for a Bolognese that can taste overwhelmingly of tomatoes.

My tomato rant notwithstanding, fruit vegetables are summer's bounty. They are at their best in summer's last hurrah — those days when the sun sinks lower but the sun still blazes.

Spurred on by courgettes, tomatoes, squash, peppers, all coming thick and fast, cooking at this time of the year has a different momentum. Must. Use. Vegetables. Faster. Exponential stockpiles of courgettes in my local fruit and vegetable shop demand a kind of flamboyance to my cookery. So prolific, I feel compelled to use them and at a gluttonous and rapid rate. Boiled whole smallish courgettes, squashed under a plate to extract the water, mixed with raw garlic, fresh mint, lemon and olive oil should easily give hummus a run for its money.

Late summer with my children, there is nothing I'd rather do than take a rummage along the vegetable patch at my mother and stepfather's house. Upending the courgettes gone stellar, waiting and watching the squash and pumpkins and, finally, patiently, picking the tomatoes. The garden is a wonderland charged with summer's opulence. For the children, the garden takes on mythical proportions, with hobgoblins, flower fairies and sprites living there under the canopy of those triffid-like leaves.

Before long, teatime will be in dusk and then dark, and summer will feel like forever ago.

FRESH TOMATOES BAKED IN CREAM

Quite possibly, this is one of the most perfect ways to cook a tomato when in season. I think it's best of all with roast chicken or lamb, and with plenty of bread to mop up the pale and creamy baked tomato juices.

~ ~ ~ ~

Serves 4

- 500g ripe tomatoes
- salt and freshly ground black pepper
- 1 tsp finely chopped fresh thyme or oregano leaves, or a couple of bay leaves
- 75ml double cream
- 1 small clove of garlic, finely chopped
- 1 tsp Dijon mustard
- 2 tbsp freshly grated Parmesan cheese
- 2 tbsp breadcrumbs

1. Preheat the oven to 200°C/gas mark 6.
2. Slice the tomatoes thickly and lay them, slightly overlapping, in a single layer in an ovenproof dish. Season with salt, pepper and the herbs.
3. Mix together the cream, garlic and mustard. Add a little extra salt if needed and pour over the tomatoes.
4. Sprinkle over the Parmesan and breadcrumbs and bake for about 30 minutes, until golden and bubbling.

FOUR
TOMATO SAUCES

A good homemade tomato sauce is essential and ever handy for a ripe burst of flavour. Make a quantity of it and keep it refrigerated or frozen in batches, on standby for pasta, pizza and to add depth and resonance to soups, stews and braises.

To cook a tomato sauce from scratch should take upwards of an hour. Soft, sweet onions, garlic and whole tinned tomatoes balanced with vinegar and a pinch of sugar, brought together with a cohesive slug of good olive oil. It takes time to craft a well-made tomato sauce. Done hastily, tinned tomatoes can taste acidic – worse still, have a 'tinny' taint to them.

Additional ingredients added to a slow-cooked tomato sauce can then give the finished sauce very different applications.

~ ~ ~ ~

Serves 4

Basic sauce
- 3 tbsp olive oil
- 1 red onion, finely diced
- 3 fat cloves of garlic, finely chopped
- 400g good, tinned whole plum tomatoes with juice
- a pinch of caster sugar
- a small splash (½ dsp) red wine vinegar
- salt and freshly ground black pepper

1. Heat 2 tablespoons of the olive oil in a saucepan on a medium-to-low heat and add the diced onion. Cook until soft and translucent – about 10 minutes. Add the chopped garlic and continue cooking for another 2 or 3 minutes, until you can smell the garlic beginning to cook in the pan. Don't let it colour or go brown.

2. Add the tomatoes, breaking them up with a wooden spoon, then add the sugar and vinegar. Season with salt and pepper.

3. Bring to a simmer, then turn the heat down to low and simmer for about 45 minutes, stirring from time to time.

4. Take the sauce off the heat and add the final spoonful of olive oil. This will soften the sauce and give it a lovely gloss. Stir and check the seasoning. The sharpness of the tomato should have abated and the sauce should taste rich and fruity and be the deepest red.

Tomato and Herb Sauce

1. Add soft herbs like basil, oregano and marjoram in generous amounts, roughly chopped, just before removing the sauce from the heat, to retain their vibrant clean flavours. These sorts of herbs don't hold their flavour if exposed to lengthy cooking. You can also scatter some of these herbs over the final dish.

2. Add a sprinkling of robust chopped herbs like rosemary, bay, savory, thyme and sage alongside the tomatoes at the beginning, as they will continue to add flavour throughout the cooking.

Tomato, Paprika and Chilli Sauce (also known as Bravas Sauce)

1. Add 1 chopped fresh red deseeded chilli or 1 teaspoon of chilli flakes alongside the garlic in the recipe opposite.

2. Then add 1 teaspoon of smoked paprika along with the tomatoes.

3. A diced green or red pepper added at the same time as the onions is a good addition.

Spiced Tomato Sauce with Cinnamon and Allspice

1. Add 1 teaspoon each of ground cinnamon and allspice to the onions just as they are finishing softening. You can use either spice alone, or both combined. A pinch of chilli flakes can be a good addition.

2. For a much subtler sauce use whole spices, fishing them out when the cooking time is complete.

3. This sauce is also very nice with a knob of butter added at the end and even a tiny drizzle of honey.

SPEEDY
TOMATO SAUCE

Because there are times when life's too short to fry an onion.

As for a speedy tomato sauce made in the time it takes to cook some pasta – there is a trick. To sidestep the lengthy cooking time necessary to balance and concentrate a whole tin of tomatoes (see page 172), drain the whole tomatoes of their juice (which is much less flavoursome and more acidic – nevertheless reserve it for use in other cooking), squeeze out the seeds and juice, and fry these whole tomatoes with olive oil, garlic and herbs, if using. It is actually necessary to omit onions when making a quick tomato sauce, as these take time to cook properly. Garlic is quite happy on its own in this speedy version of a tomato sauce.

~ ~ ~ ~

Serves 4

- 3 tbsp olive oil
- 3 fat cloves of garlic, finely chopped
- 1 x 400g tin of whole plum tomatoes, drained well of juice
- salt and freshly ground black pepper

1. Place a large non-stick frying pan on a moderate heat and add 2 tablespoons of the olive oil. The wider the surface area to cook the tomatoes, the better. Maximum exposure to the heat is necessary for the sauce to cook speedily.

2. Add the garlic and cook, stirring with a wooden spoon, until it JUST begins to soften. Don't let it brown – when you can smell the garlic beginning to cook in the pan, add the whole drained tomatoes and mash them down with the back of a wooden spoon. Add salt and pepper to taste.

3. Bring to a rapid simmer, then turn the heat down and simmer for 5–10 minutes to concentrate the flavours. Add the final spoonful of olive oil to round the sauce off and give it gloss.

TOMATO
KETCHUP

Ask at your vegetable shop if they are able to get hold of a box of 'seconds' for you. These tomatoes are often a little over-ripe and all the better for making tomato ketchup with.

~ ~ ~ ~

Makes 1 litre

- 4kg ripe red tomatoes, roughly chopped
- 2 medium onions, finely chopped
- 4 cloves of garlic, finely sliced
- 250ml cider vinegar
- 150ml malt vinegar
- 200g light muscovado sugar
- 1 tbsp sea salt flakes
- 1 tsp English mustard
- 1 heaped tsp ground cloves
- 1 tsp ground allspice
- ½ tsp ground ginger
- 1 cinnamon stick
- 1 heaped tsp celery salt
- 1 tsp ground white pepper

1. Put the tomatoes, onion and garlic into a large heavy-based pan. Add the vinegars, sugar and the rest of the ingredients and bring to the boil, making sure you stir all the while to dissolve the sugar. Cover with a lid. Reduce the heat to the merest blip and cook for a further 3–3½ hours. Be vigilant: you don't want the sauce to stick on the bottom and the ingredients to catch – stir vigorously from time to time.

2. When ready, the mixture should be well cooked and integrated and very pulpy in appearance. Take off the heat and remove the cinnamon stick.

3. Blitz the mixture in a blender until smooth.

4. Ladle through a fine sieve into a clean saucepan. Use the back of the ladle to really push the mixture through the sieve and squeeze out every last drop. Discard the skin and pip debris in the sieve only when you are sure you have pushed through all the liquid.

5. Bring the sieved sauce to a lively simmer and taste and adjust the seasoning as you see fit – salt, pepper, perhaps even a splodge more sugar? The mixture will spit and bubble. Be careful and heat like this for 2–3 minutes, stirring continuously.

6. Meanwhile, sterilize some freshly cleaned bottles in a warm oven (180°C/gas mark 4) for 10 minutes. Ensure the stoppers are washed thoroughly. Ideally, try to get your hands on some of those fancy drink bottles with stoppers fastened on by a piece of metal.

7. Using a funnel, pour the hot sauce into the warm sterilized bottles and leave for 30 minutes with the odd bottle bump to dislodge any bubbles. Seal accordingly and store in a cupboard for a month or so before using. Once opened, store in the fridge.

TURLU TURLU

A dish with Turkish heritage, turlu turlu basically translates as 'a mixture', a hotchpotch, and that's exactly what this is. Roasted and spiced vegetables with chickpeas, tomatoes and herbs, it's a hop and a skip from France's ratatouille (see page 178). Try to prepare all the vegetables to a similar size, the exception being the garlic. Turlu turlu is best served warm or at room temperature, and never piping hot.

~ ~ ~ ~

Serves 4

- 3 large potatoes, peeled and cubed
- 2 carrots, peeled and diced
- 1 onion, diced
- ½ tsp ground allspice
- 1 tbsp whole coriander seeds, toasted (see page 12)
- salt and freshly ground black pepper
- 6 tbsp olive oil
- 2 cloves of garlic, sliced
- 1 aubergine, cubed
- 2 courgettes, diced
- 2 peppers (any colour), deseeded and diced
- 200g spiced tomato sauce with cinnamon and allspice (see page 173)
- 250g cooked or tinned chickpeas, drained of their liquid
- 1 large bunch of fresh coriander leaves, chopped

To serve

- 200g plain yoghurt, seasoned with salt and garlic (see page 10)
- 1 tsp chilli flakes (optional)

1. Preheat the oven to 200°C/gas mark 6.

2. In a large roasting tin, combine the potatoes, carrots and onions with half the allspice and coriander seeds, a pinch of salt and half the olive oil. Roast for 20 minutes. Remove the tin from the oven and turn all the vegetables over in the pan. Roast for a further 20 minutes, until completely cooked and tender, then remove from the roasting tin and put the cooked vegetables to one side in a wide serving dish.

3. In the same roasting tin, combine the garlic, aubergine, courgettes and peppers with the rest of the allspice and coriander seeds, a pinch of salt and the remaining olive oil. Roast for 10 minutes, then remove the tin from the oven, turn all the vegetables over and roast for another 5–10 minutes. These vegetables need to be tender and cooked but not mushy. Add to the other vegetables in the serving dish.

4. Heat up the tomato sauce and taste for seasoning. Gently fold half the warm sauce into the vegetables in the serving dish. Add the cooked chickpeas.

5. To serve, top the turlu turlu with the remaining tomato sauce and the chopped coriander. Spoon over some seasoned yoghurt and sprinkle with chilli flakes, if using.

RATATOUILLE

All things bright and ... ratatouille.

Served warm or at room temperature, ratatouille is great. It is important to cook each vegetable individually. I want the onions melted and sweet, the courgettes to have caught in the pan ever so slightly at their edges but still have bite, the peppers to be slippery and luscious and the aubergines creamy and soft. If you cook the vegetables all together in a pan, the individual merits of each vegetable are lost and the result is more like a vegetable stew.

~ ~ ~ ~

Serves 4
- 2 onions, roughly chopped
- olive oil, for cooking
- 4 cloves of garlic, thinly sliced
- 2 aubergines, halved lengthways and cut into chunky cubes
- 2 red peppers, deseeded and cut into eighths
- 4 small courgettes, thickly sliced into rounds
- 1 quantity of tomato sauce with basil (see page 173)
- salt and freshly ground black pepper
- 2 tbsp fresh thyme leaves
- 10 large fresh basil leaves, to serve

1. Preheat the oven to 180°C/gas mark 4.
2. Cook the onions in a little olive oil in a frying pan over a moderate heat until they are soft, sweet and beginning to turn golden (about 10 minutes). Add the garlic and cook for a further 3–4 minutes, until soft. Remove the onions and garlic from the pan and reserve on a plate.
3. Put the frying pan back over a high heat, add a little more olive oil and fry the aubergines (in batches if necessary) until golden brown and cooked through. You may need to lower the heat after a minute, but start off high so the aubergines do not soak up too much of the oil. Drain the aubergines in a sieve and add to the plate of onions.
4. Wipe the pan and add a little more olive oil. Add the peppers and cook until soft, with wrinkly, blistered skin. Add the peppers to the waiting plate of cooked vegetables.
5. Wipe out the pan again, then fry the courgettes over a moderate heat in a little more olive oil until they have singed slightly around their edges and are cooked, though still with a slight bite.
6. Warm the tomato sauce gently in a wide ovenproof pan for a minute or so, then gently fold into the vegetable mix, seasoning with salt, black pepper and the thyme leaves.
7. Bake in the oven for about 10 minutes, so that the flavours meld together. You want the vegetables to be soft and tender, but certainly not mushy. Add the basil and set aside for 10 or so minutes before serving.

SQUASHED
COURGETTES

Serves 4 as a side dish

- 500g smallish courgettes
  (big ones are too watery
  and will not squash nicely)
- salt and freshly ground
  black pepper
- 5 tbsp extra-virgin olive oil
- ½ a clove of garlic, crushed
- juice and zest of ½ a lemon,
  or more to taste

To serve

- 1 small bunch of fresh herbs, leaves
  picked (mint, dill or basil are best)
- chilli flakes, (optional)

1. Bring a large pan of water to a steady boil. Add the courgettes and a generous pinch of salt. Don't cram them in too tightly, as they need room to roll around and boil. Cook for about 20 minutes on a gentle boil. Near the end of the cooking time, check for doneness by lifting one courgette from the water with a large slotted spoon or spatula. It should be soft enough to droop a bit from the end of the spoon but the courgette should not break apart.

2. When ready, remove the courgettes to a colander and let them cool for a few minutes. Now press the courgettes in the colander, using quite a heavy weight placed on top of a plate that fits neatly over them. Allow the courgettes to drain under the weight for about 20 minutes or more.

3. Remove the weight, then take the courgettes out of the colander and roughly chop them on a board. Season with salt.

4. Put the courgettes into a bowl and add 4 tablespoons of olive oil, the garlic, lemon juice and zest. Check the seasoning.

5. To serve, spread the squashed courgettes out on a large plate and scatter over the herbs, chilli flakes (if using) and the remaining spoonful of olive oil.

COURGETTE
LOAF

A recipe from my Kiwi mother-in-law, Mary – flecked green with courgettes, best eaten sliced cold and spread with butter.

~ ~ ~ ~

Makes two 900g loaves

- 220g grated courgette
  (2 courgettes, roughly)
- 350g caster sugar
- 225ml sunflower oil
- 3 eggs
- 1 vanilla pod, scraped of seeds,
  or 1 tsp vanilla extract
- 330g self-raising flour
- ¼ tsp baking powder
- 1 tsp ground cinnamon
- 1 tsp bicarbonate of soda
- ½ tsp salt (optional)
- 80g raisins or chopped dates

1. Preheat the oven to 160°C/gas mark 3. Grease two 900g loaf tins and line them with baking parchment.
2. In a mixing bowl, beat together the grated courgette, the sugar, oil, eggs and vanilla extract.
3. Sift the flour, baking powder, cinnamon, bicarbonate of soda and salt (if using) into the wet mixture. Mix together and add the raisins or dates.
4. Pour the mixture into the prepared tins and bake for 1 hour, or until a skewer comes out clean when inserted into the centre.
5. Leave to cool in the tins, then turn out on a wire rack to finish cooling.

WHOLEMEAL PUMPKIN, FETA & YOGHURT MUFFINS

Makes 6–8 large muffins

- 90g unsalted butter, plus extra for greasing
- 225g wholewheat flour (plain if you'd rather)
- 1 tsp baking powder
- ½ tsp salt (optional)
- 75g cooked cubed pumpkin or squash (any leftover roasted pumpkin from a previous meal would be ideal, but by all means cook fresh if needed)
- 75g feta cheese, crumbled into pieces
- 50g pumpkin or sunflower seeds (optional)
- 1 dsp caraway seeds, toasted (see page 12)
- 1 egg
- 175g plain yoghurt

1. Preheat the oven to 200°C/gas mark 6.
2. Butter the moulds of a large 6-hole muffin tin.
3. Sift the flour, baking powder and salt into a large mixing bowl, adding any bran residue from the sieve for wholemeal flour.
4. Add the cooked pumpkin, crumbled feta, pumpkin or sunflower seeds and toasted caraway seeds to the bowl.
5. Over a low heat, melt the butter in a pan (or microwave).
6. Combine the egg, yoghurt and melted butter in a separate bowl.
7. Add the egg, yoghurt and butter mix to the other ingredients and gently stir to combine. The less mixing, the better.
8. Divide the mix between the muffin moulds – each portion about the size of a satsuma.
9. Bake for 20–25 minutes, until golden brown and crisp on top and springy to the touch.
10. Best of all eaten while warm.

DEEP-FRIED PUMPKIN WITH HONEY & LABNEH

A showstopper of a dish. Children (and adults) will love the addition of honey and soft creamy labneh to the hot battered pumpkin.

Deep-frying does pose a danger. After frying, be sure to leave the hot oil to cool down somewhere safe and out of the reach of children. Strain the used oil and reserve to use another time.

~ ~ ~ ~

Serves 4 as a side or snack

- 500g pumpkin or squash, peeled and deseeded
- 150ml ice-cold water
- 100g chickpea (gram) flour
- salt
- 400–800ml vegetable oil, depending on the size of your pan

To serve

- ½ recipe of labneh (see page 20), or thick Greek yoghurt, or curd cheese
- 2 tbsp runny honey
- 1 tsp dried oregano
- ½ tsp chilli flakes

1. Cut the pumpkin or squash into thin slices (each about 2–3mm thick).
2. Quickly whisk the water into the flour and add ½ teaspoon of salt.
3. Put the oil into a deep heavy-based saucepan, making sure it is no more than one-third full. Heat the oil to 180°C (or until a cube of bread sizzles and turns brown when dropped into it).
4. Dip the pumpkin slices in the batter and fry in batches for about 5 minutes until golden brown on each side.
5. Drain on kitchen paper and keep warm until you have fried enough to serve.
6. Serve the pumpkin pieces on a plate with the labneh, drizzled with a thin stream of honey, and sprinkle over some oregano, chilli flakes and a little more salt if you like.

ROOT VEGETABLES

Roooooot vegetables, tubers too. Winter's ascent spurs thoughts of hunkering down, roasting, toasting, gnarled-knobbled, beautiful-ugly, the muted hues of many vegetables so different from those green jewels of summer.

No surprise then that I look forward to the year's end: my cooking of vegetables does an about-turn and focuses on those beauties grown beneath the ground. Breathtaking are those early icy mornings spent following the first footprints of Jack Frost. That this cold improves some root vegetables and brassicas is a happy fact. Converting starches to sugar to prevent themselves from freezing, these vegetables taste all the sweeter after a frost or two.

Cream, butter and cheese, happy with all roots and tubers, make these vegetables a luxurious and nourishing wintry staple. And when all that rich, unctuous and (dare I say it?) fatty cooking begins to wear thin, off I'll head to the mezzes of the eastern Mediterranean and Middle East or perhaps one of those tangy New York-style slaws. Emboldened by spice in a pilaf or grated raw for a perky salad, these vegetables lend an earthy sweetness to my cooking.

PATATAS BRAVAS

Serves 4 (alongside other mezze)

- 450g potatoes, peeled
  and cut into 2–3cm chunks
- a good 4 tbsp of olive oil, plus
  extra for greasing
- fine sea salt
- 1 recipe of Bravas sauce
  (see page 173)

1. Preheat the oven to 200°C/gas mark 6.
2. Arrange the potatoes in a single layer in an oiled roasting tin. Liberally drizzle them with enough oil to coat well, and sprinkle with salt.
3. Bake until golden and crisp – about 45 minutes.
4. Heat the bravas sauce and spoon on to a wide serving plate or bowl. Place the hot roasted potatoes on top of the sauce and serve immediately.

CELERIAC REMOULADE

I love celeriac. It's like nutty, sweet celery. Peeled and served raw, this rhino-skinned root vegetable is a classic French salad offering. I find crème fraîche lighter and less claggy than mayonnaise. The stark whiteness of this wintry salad sits well alongside some ham and perhaps a baked potato.

Serves 4

- 1 celeriac, peeled and cut into very
  thin matchsticks or coarsely grated
- salt and freshly ground black pepper
- juice of 1 lemon
- 200g crème fraîche
- 2 tbsp Dijon mustard

1. Place the cut or grated celeriac in a large colander and add a generous pinch of salt to help extract excess moisture and soften the vegetable. Squeeze over and stir in the juice of half the lemon to stop the celeriac discolouring; leave for 10 minutes.
2. In a bowl, mix the crème fraîche, mustard, and the juice from the remaining half lemon with a pinch of salt.
3. Give the celeriac a good squeeze, add salt and pepper to taste and place in a serving dish. Mix the dressing into the celeriac and serve.

BEETROOT & YOGHURT

Serves 4

- 500g cooked and peeled beetroot, cut into chunks
- 1 clove of garlic, peeled
- 2 tsp cumin seeds, roasted and ground (see page 12)
- 1 tbsp red wine vinegar or balsamic vinegar, or to taste
- 3 tbsp extra-virgin olive oil
- 1 small bunch of dill, roughly chopped
- 100g plain yoghurt
- salt

1. Place the beetroot in a blender with the garlic, cumin, vinegar, 2 tablespoons of oil and all but about 1 tablespoon of the chopped dill. Blend to an utterly smooth purée.

2. Add the yoghurt and pulse quickly, once or twice, to amalgamate.

3. Add salt to taste. You may also need a few more drops of vinegar if you want a sharper purée.

4. Spoon out into a shallow serving bowl or plate.

5. Top with the reserved chopped dill and the remaining tablespoon of olive oil.

6. Serve with flatbreads or breadsticks. This beetroot purée is also very nice studded with pieces of feta cheese on top.

CHAMP

Serves 4 as a side dish

- 1.2kg floury potatoes, peeled and cut into equal-size pieces
- salt and freshly ground black pepper
- 80–100g butter
- 1 bunch of spring onions, finely chopped
- 200ml warm milk

1. Cook the potatoes in boiling salted water for 20 minutes or until tender. Drain well.
2. Put the pan back on a moderate heat and melt the butter, then add the spring onions and gently fry for 5 minutes or until just tender. Remove with a slotted spoon and put to one side. Return the potatoes to the pan along with the oniony butter.
3. Mash the potatoes well, beat in the warm milk, stir in the spring onions and season with salt and pepper.

CARROT & SWEDE MASH

I like this mash to have a bit of texture to it, so use a stick blender or a masher; but if you prefer it completely smooth, use a food processor.

Serves 4 generously as a side

- 3 large carrots, peeled and diced into ice-cube-sized pieces
- 1 swede, peeled and diced into ice-cube-sized pieces
- salt and freshly ground black pepper
- 1 sprig of fresh thyme
- 75ml milk
- 75g butter
- freshly grated nutmeg, to taste

1. Put the carrots and swede into a pan and cover with water. Add a pinch of salt and the thyme sprig. Bring to the boil, then cover the pan and cook for 20 minutes or until tender. Drain well in a colander, allowing the vegetables to steam until quite dry.
2. Return the pan to a low heat with the milk and butter. Add salt, pepper and nutmeg, then put the carrots and swede back into the pan and cook, mashing the vegetables with a stick blender or potato masher, until you have the texture you like. Taste for seasoning and serve. The mash will keep warm quite happily for a while before the meal.

ONION RINGS

Makes as many as there are rings in an onion

- vegetable oil, for deep-frying
- 150g self-raising flour
- salt and freshly ground black pepper
- 200ml very cold soda or fizzy water
- 1 large onion, thinly sliced into rounds

1. Heat the oil to 180°C in a deep-fat fryer. Alternatively, half fill a heavy-based saucepan with oil and heat until a bread cube takes 1 minute to fry and turn golden brown and crisp in the oil – this will tell you if the oil in the pan is hot enough.

2. Put the flour into a bowl with a pinch of salt, then quickly whisk in the cold soda water until you have a thick paste. Don't overmix it, and make it just before you fry the onion rings.

3. Position the bowl of batter next to the fryer or pan. Have a plate lined with kitchen paper ready. Dip your onion rings into the batter, then carefully drop them into the oil, shaking the basket (or stirring carefully with a slotted spoon) to prevent the rings sticking. Don't overcrowd the fryer or pan. Fry for 2–3 minutes until crisp and golden.

4. Remove from the oil and drain on kitchen paper. Season with extra salt and some pepper as you like. Serve straight away.

CARROT & ALMOND CAKE

This fabulous cake is based on the one in *Jane Grigson's Vegetable Book,* here with a little less sugar.

~ ~ ~ ~

Makes one 20cm cake
- 4 eggs, separated
- 180g caster sugar
- 250g ground almonds
- 250g carrots, peeled and finely grated
- 1 heaped tbsp self-raising flour
- 70g pine nuts

1. Preheat the oven to 180°C/gas mark 4 and line a 20cm round cake tin with greaseproof paper.
2. Whisk the egg whites until stiff in a very clean bowl with a clean whisk.
3. Beat the egg yolks and sugar together with a sturdy whisk for about 5 minutes.
4. Mix the almonds, carrots and flour into the egg yolk mixture, then gently fold in the egg whites and pour into the prepared cake tin.
5. Scatter with pine nuts and bake for about 40 minutes, until a skewer comes out clean and the cake is springy to touch. Allow to cool a bit, then remove from the tin and cool on a wire rack.

BEETROOT & CHOCOLATE CAKE

Cooked beetroot moistens the cake crumb. It also adds an earthy and discreet sweetness to the cocoa powder.

~ ~ ~ ~

Makes one 20cm cake

- 200ml vegetable oil, plus extra for greasing
- 100g rice flour
- 100g ground almonds
- 1 tsp bicarbonate of soda
- 75g cocoa powder
- 250g caster sugar
- 250g cooked and peeled beetroot (about 4 small ones)
- 3 eggs

1. Preheat the oven to 180°C/gas mark 4. Grease and line a 20cm round cake tin with baking parchment.
2. Mix the rice flour, ground almonds, bicarbonate of soda, cocoa powder and sugar in a large bowl.
3. Purée the beetroot in a food processor or blender, then add the eggs one at a time, whizzing between each addition.
4. Pour in the oil and process until smooth.
5. Add the beetroot mixture to the dry ingredients and mix to combine.
6. Pour into the prepared tin and bake for about 40 minutes, or until a skewer inserted into the centre of the cake comes out clean and the cake is firm to touch.
7. Cool in the tin for 5 minutes, then remove from the tin and place on a wire rack to cool completely.

GREEN VEGETABLES

Vegetables or fruit: for the rest of your life, what's it to be? This is a question often bandied about my kitchen. For me, without a doubt, it would be vegetables. So absolute is my fervour for veg, I've written three chapters in order to cram in more and more vegetable recipes. If this book keeps growing, snowball style, it's all down to vegetables.

What frustrates me most when it comes to feeding children is that the calls to 'eat your veg' so often go unanswered. Fact: if vegetables are served unadorned and growing cold on the side of the plate, the journey from fork to waiting child's mouth might as well be a quarrelsome one.

Integrate those vegetables. Cook them in among and flatter them alongside other components of the dish. Not only will those vegetables begin to be tolerated, but I dare say they will be eaten with enthusiasm. Embrace the concept of introducing vegetables by stealth. Teatime squabbles about vegetable demolition will soon turn on their head. A cauliflower cooked slowly and almost to a pulp with fennel seeds and garlic, given a squeeze of lemon and served warm stuffed in pitta breads, makes a sumptuous lunch that all children will love.

Likewise, I doubt there is a better way to get more broccoli per capita into a child than to serve what my children reverentially call 'broccoli pesto pasta' (see page 99). I've an inkling that (always said quickly) 'pestopasta' would be in the top three suppers of all children; although this broccoli-dominant dish actually has no pesto in it whatsoever, the name makes it sound reassuringly normal to their friends. With the bit between my teeth, I'm keen to demonstrate that flavour is there at the tips of your fingers and need not be something you spoon from a jar.

Vegetables dominate in the food I cook, week in, week out. That my children eat plenty of them is down to their sheer deliciousness.

GREEN BEANS
WITH TOMATO & BASIL

This tangle of purposely overcooked beans with with tomato and basil (black olives are magnificent here, too) is delicious. Best eaten warm or room temperature and as an accompaniment to just about anything.

~ ~ ~ ~

Serves 4 as a side dish

- 400g green beans, trimmed
- 1 recipe of tomato sauce
  with basil (see page 173)
- 1 small bunch of fresh basil, roughly
  chopped (marjoram, parsley, oregano
  and dill have all worked well too)
- 2 tbsp extra-virgin olive oil
- a large pinch of chilli
  flakes (optional)
- salt and freshly ground black pepper

1. First cook your beans in plenty of salted boiling water. You want them cooked through and tender, about 8–10 minutes. Remove from the heat and drain.
2. Heat the tomato sauce in a pan over a moderate heat and add the cooked beans.
3. Warm the beans in the tomato sauce for a minute or two. Stir in the basil, olive oil and the chilli flakes, if using, and add salt and pepper to taste.

~ ~ ~ ~ ~ ~ ~ ~ ~ ~ ~ ~

FENNEL BULB &
SEED YOGHURT

A fennel tzatziki, if you like. Serve as a dip with warm flatbread, or with grilled meat and fish.

~ ~ ~ ~

Makes a good bowlful

- 1 small fennel bulb, with plenty
  of feathery fronds
- 300g plain yoghurt
- 1 clove of garlic
- ½ tsp salt
- juice of ½–1 lemon
- 1 tsp fennel seeds, toasted
  and crushed (see page 12)

1. Trim the fennel by removing the tough stalks (reserve the fronds).
2. Halve the bulb lengthwise and discard the very hard central core. Grate the fennel using a box grater and stir into the yoghurt. Add the chopped fronds.
3. Crush the garlic with the salt and add to the yoghurt with the lemon juice, to taste, and ground fennel seeds.
4. The fennel yoghurt will keep well, covered, in the fridge for up to 3 days.

ROASTED ASPARAGUS

Granted, the first tender spears of the asparagus season require little else other than a brief boil and some melted butter to serve. But as the spears come thick, fast and cheaper towards the end of their short UK growing season, I think it's nice to experiment. Roasted in a fierce oven or on the barbecue, the asparagus wizens in the heat and sucks up any extra flavour.

~ ~ ~ ~

Serves 4 as a starter

- 1kg asparagus
- 4 tbsp olive oil
- salt and freshly ground black pepper
- 1 clove of garlic, finely chopped
- juice of ½ a lemon
- 1 small bunch of fresh basil, leaves roughly chopped

1. Preheat the oven to its maximum heat – 240°C+/gas mark 9.
2. Trim the asparagus by gently bending the base of each stem until it snaps at the natural breaking point. Discard the woody ends, and wash and dry the asparagus spears.
3. In a large bowl, mix the asparagus gently with half the olive oil, coating the stalks. Add salt, pepper and the garlic and mix.
4. Lay the spears in a single layer in a roasting tin and roast in the oven for 12–15 minutes, until blistered and soft – you don't want them al dente.
5. To the bowl, add the remaining oil with the lemon juice and basil.
6. Remove the asparagus from the oven and, while still very hot, tip the spears into the bowl. Mix well and check for seasoning.
7. Serve warm or cold, as you like.

~ ~ ~ ~ ~ ~ ~ ~ ~ ~ ~ ~ ~

SPINACH DIFFERENTLY

Spinach cooked here with onions, garlic, raisins and spice – makes the green stuff really sing.

~ ~ ~ ~

Serves 4 as a side dish

- 3 tbsp extra-virgin olive oil
- 1 small onion, finely diced
- 3 cloves of garlic, thinly sliced
- 50g raisins
- 50g pine nuts or chopped almonds, lightly toasted (see page 64)
- a good pinch of toasted and ground cumin seeds (see page 12)
- a good pinch of smoked paprika
- sea salt and black pepper
- 300g spinach leaves, washed and dried

1. Heat the olive oil in a large frying pan. Add the onion and garlic and cook until absolutely soft and turning golden.
2. Add the raisins and pine nuts and stir to combine.
3. Add the ground spices, salt and freshly ground pepper to taste.
4. Add spinach and toss the leaves until wilted and cooked.
5. Serve – especially nice with fish, chicken or lamb.

LAO-STYLE PORK, NOODLE & LETTUCE WRAPS

Interactive family eating; a little bit of this and a little bit of that. Here in the green vegetables section because of all that lovely buttery lettuce.

~ ~ ~ ~

Serves 4

- 100g dried vermicelli noodles
- 2 tbsp vegetable oil
- 3 cloves of garlic, finely chopped
- 500g minced pork
- 1 thumb-size piece of unpeeled fresh root ginger, grated
- 1 lemongrass blade, finely chopped
- 2 tbsp light soy sauce
- 1 tbsp XO sauce (optional – you can use ½ tbsp soft brown sugar if you'd rather)
- ½ tbsp sesame oil
- 2 tbsp fish sauce

To serve

- 1 cucumber, peeled, deseeded and thinly sliced
- 1 large carrot, peeled and grated
- 1 small bunch of spring onions, finely sliced
- 2 heads of soft-leaf lettuce, washed and separated into individual leaves
- 1 small bunch of fresh mint, leaves chopped
- 1 small bunch of fresh coriander, leaves chopped
- 150g peanuts, roasted (see page 77), then chopped or crushed
- sweet chilli sauce
- 2 limes, cut into wedges

1. Put the noodles into a pan and pour boiling water over them. Let them soak for 15 minutes, or until soft, then refresh them in cold water and drain in a colander.

2. Place a frying pan over a medium heat. Add the vegetable oil and the garlic and cook for a minute or so. Don't let the garlic brown.

3. Turn up the heat and add the minced pork. Cook for about a minute, stirring it around the pan and breaking it up.

4. Add the ginger, lemongrass, soy sauce, XO sauce (or sugar), sesame oil and fish sauce. Mix well to coat the mince and continue to cook for 5–10 minutes until all the pork is lightly browned and any pan juices have begun to evaporate.

5. Using a slotted spoon, remove the cooked pork to a serving dish, leaving the fat behind in the pan.

6. To serve, have the noodles, mince (warm or room temperature), salads, herbs and nuts in different serving bowls on the table, with the chilli sauce and lime wedges.

7. Using a leaf of lettuce as the wrap, add a forkful of noodles, a spoonful of pork mix, cucumber, spring onion, carrot, chopped fresh herbs, peanuts and chilli sauce as you go.

8. Serve with wedges of lime to squeeze over.

VARIATION: NOODLE SALAD

Alternatively, shred the lettuce, put into a big bowl with all the other ingredients and serve as a noodle salad.

SAUERKRAUT

Quite apart from this being the one thing I craved above all while pregnant, I'm very glad this pickled-cabbage addiction has now passed on to my children and it wasn't just in utero. We buy jars of sauerkraut from our local Polish grocery store. Forked straight from the jar and added to a grilled cheese sandwich with grainy mustard, it's a quick fix, but for ultimate pickled-cabbage fix, braised with smoked meat and crème fraîche in the French style of choucroute garnie – I dare say there's no better way to eat cabbage.

~ ~ ~ ~

Serves 4

For the base
- 20g butter
- 100g smoked streaky bacon, finely diced
- 1 large carrot, peeled and finely diced
- 1 large onion, finely diced
- 1 clove of garlic, finely diced
- 1 x 500g jar of sauerkraut
- 750ml ham or chicken stock (see page 165 and 145)
- aromatics – very flexible but the following are perfect: 15 coriander seeds, 10 juniper berries, 2 bay leaves, a few fresh parsley stalks
- salt and freshly ground white or black pepper
- sugar or honey, to taste

To serve
- 400g chunks of cooked smoked (or unsmoked) ham hock meat (see page 165) and/or cooked smoked or unsmoked sausage, or any combination of cured hams and sausages (charcuterie)
- 4 tbsp crème fraîche
- a small bunch of fresh parsley, leaves finely chopped

1. Heat the butter in a pan, add the bacon and gently sauté for 5 minutes or until very lightly coloured. Add the carrot, onion and garlic and cook until soft and sweet, but not coloured, about 5 minutes. Add the sauerkraut and stir well.

2. Add the stock and the aromatics. Cover with a cartouche (a sheet of greaseproof or baking paper cut into a circle just larger than the pan, run under a tap, gently scrunched up and unfolded to cover the contents of the pan snugly).

3. Return the pan to the heat and gently braise the sauerkraut for 10–15 minutes until the liquid has just about evaporated. Finish by checking the seasoning, adding salt, pepper and sugar or honey to taste.

4. To serve, heat the meats through in the sauerkraut mixture for a few minutes, then stir in the crème fraîche and parsley. Serve piping hot.

SLOW-COOKED CAULIFLOWER

Serves 4 as a side dish

- salt
- 2 medium cauliflowers, broken up into satsuma-size florets, pale inner leaves reserved
- 80ml olive oil
- 5 cloves of garlic, finely sliced
- 2 tsp fennel seeds
- 2 handfuls of parsley, leaves roughly chopped
- ½ tsp red chilli flakes (optional)
- juice and zest of ½ a lemon

1. Put a large pan of salted water on the heat and bring to the boil. Add the cauliflower and boil for 2 minutes. Drain, then return the pan to the heat and add the olive oil.

2. Over a medium heat, add the cauliflower and garlic and season with a little salt. Give the pan a good stir and put a lid on. Turn the heat to very low and cook for 10 minutes.

3. Remove the lid, add the fennel seeds, stir and put back the lid. Cook for a further 20 minutes, stirring and scraping from time to time and always keeping the temperature as low as possible. The cauliflower is ready when it is very soft and falling apart. Try to keep some small chunks of cauliflower in the mix – you don't want it to be too pulpy, a little texture is nice.

4. Add the parsley, chilli flakes and the lemon juice and zest. Check the seasoning and serve at room temperature.

~ ~ ~ ~ ~ ~ ~ ~ ~ ~ ~ ~

BUBBLE & SQUEAK

Audible is the squeak when I say I'll make it. This dish always makes me want to cook extra potatoes and greens, reserving a little bit of this and a little of that so that I can make it for my children.

~ ~ ~ ~

Quantities will depend on what you have available

- leftover cooked potatoes, at room temperature
- leftover cooked or freshly cooked spring greens (or cabbage or kale), roughly equal in volume to the potatoes
- salt and freshly ground black pepper
- butter

1. Mash the potatoes with a fork. Shred the leftover or freshly cooked greens and mix with the potato. Check the seasoning, adding salt and pepper to taste, then shape into flattened patties.

2. Melt some butter (a tablespoon should do) in a non-stick frying pan and when it foams add the potato patties. Don't crowd the pan. Press down gently, then leave to fry over a moderate heat for few minutes until a nice golden crust has formed. Turn over and cook the underside the same way. Repeat if you have more patties.

3. Serve. We like to eat bubble and squeak with bacon and fried eggs for a lazy late brunch.

CHARD BÖREK

Inspired by the filled Turkish pastries, these make an excellent packed lunch addition.

~ ~ ~ ~

Makes 6 Börek

For the filling
- 2 medium onions, finely chopped
- 3 tbsp olive oil
- a pinch of salt
- 2 cloves of garlic, finely sliced
- 1 tbsp mixed ground spice (allspice, black pepper, cumin, coriander, nutmeg and cinnamon work well)
- 50g pine nuts, lightly toasted (see page 64)
- 75g raisins, plumped in a little warm water and drained
- 300g chopped chard or spinach leaves
- 150g fresh or brined halloumi (see page 23), crumbled or grated
- ½ a small lemon

To assemble
- 18 fresh or defrosted frozen filo sheets
- 75g melted butter

1. First make the filling. In a large frying pan or saucepan, cook the onions in half the olive oil with a pinch of salt for 2–3 minutes until soft and translucent. Add the garlic and cook for 2–3 minutes until just turning golden, but don't let it brown.

2. Stir in the spice mix, pine nuts and soaked raisins. Scrape the onion mix on to a plate and return the pan to the heat with the rest of the olive oil.

3. Add the chopped greens to the pan and cook, turning often, until wilted, then drain in a colander.

4. Mix the spiced onions with the greens and allow to cool.

5. Add the cheese and lemon juice and check the mix for seasoning.

6. Next assemble the börek. Preheat the oven to 180°C/gas mark 4 and line a baking tray with greaseproof paper.

7. Keep the remaining sheets of filo pastry covered with a clean damp tea towel while you work so they don't dry out. Any you don't use can be stored, well wrapped, in the fridge for a few days.

8. Place 1 sheet of filo on your work surface with the longer edge at the bottom – landscape view. Brush lightly with melted butter and lay another sheet on top. Repeat with a third sheet. Cut the pastry lengthways into 3 strips.

9. Place a heaped tablespoon of filling in the bottom corner of each filo strip and fold diagonally, creating a triangle at the tip of the strip. Continue folding, following the triangular shape, leaving the final join on the bottom of the pastry.

10. Brush the top of the pastry lightly with butter and place on the prepared baking tray. Continue to make more börek with the remaining pastry and chard spinach filling.

11. Bake for 20–25 minutes, until golden and crisp. These can be prepared some time ahead before baking.

SLAW

Slaw is the American diminutive for coleslaw. I like the name and think this rebranding of a classic a good thing. The sometime salad offering of shredded carrot, cabbage and onion, barely discernible from the mayonnaise that binds it, is hardly the apex of nourishment. So slaw, with its new-fangled (deep breath), trendy connotations, is simply a great way to assemble raw vegetables. This version is lighter, swapping the mayonnaise for a perky mix of crème fraîche and lemon. The addition of sliced pear and apple and some toasted seeds in among the melee of vegetables makes it especially popular with my children.

~ ~ ~ ~

Serves 4
- ¼ of a small white cabbage, finely shredded
- ¼ of a radicchio, finely shredded
- juice of ½ a lemon
- 2 apples, unpeeled, sliced thin and cut into matchsticks (squeeze some of the lemon juice over to stop the fruit browning)
- 2 pears, unpeeled, sliced thin and cut into matchsticks (with lemons juice squeezed over as above)
- 1 small bunch of fresh flat-leaf parsley, leaves roughly chopped
- 4 spring onions, finely sliced
- 2 tbsp sesame seeds, toasted (see page 12)
- 2 tbsp crème fraîche
- salt and freshly ground black pepper

1. Assemble all the ingredients in a bowl, giving them a good mix with your hands to ensure everything is evenly coated in the crème fraîche.
2. Season with salt and pepper as you like.

GÖZLEME

On holiday in northern Cyprus a few summers back, we stopped for lunch in the sleepy village of Büyükkonuk. A perfect spot if ever there was one – sitting there in the shade of the fig tree drinking strong thick black coffee. Through the open kitchen window, I could see the chef, a Turkish-Cypriot woman, kneading the most enormous pile of dough. I went over to have a closer look.

Into the dough she added a quantity of plain yoghurt – not an ingredient I had, until now, ever seen included in a bread dough. The yoghurt, she explained, would stop the flatbreads, or gözleme, from becoming too brittle. When I asked about the ratio of yoghurt to flour to yeast to water she just laughed. And that, in a nutshell, is what's so tremendous about cooking. She couldn't and wouldn't tell me exact quantities. Back in the UK, my flour would be different, my yeast might be older/younger; she was using goat's yoghurt and most probably I would use cow's; it was much warmer in that kitchen in late August than it is in mine on a chilly February morning. You can't learn a recipe. You must make one. And then make it your own.

With the dough proven for an hour or so until doubled in size, she pulled off satsuma-size pieces of the dough and rolled them vigorously until cardboard thin and oval-shaped. On to one half she grated halloumi and sprinkled dried mint. Folding the oval together and squishing the seams tight shut, she put the flatbreads to cook on a hot, dry cast-iron griddle pan.

Her gözleme were memorable. I think the children probably ate their own body weight in those crisp warm flatbreads that afternoon. I don't have a fig tree to sit under outside, but with my eyes tight shut, I can almost feel the sunshine on my back when I make these for tea.

Makes 8–10 flatbreads

For the dough
- 500g plain flour, plus extra for dusting
- 5g salt
- 1 level tsp dried yeast (about 4g)
- 225ml cold water
- 150g plain yoghurt
- olive oil, for kneading

For the filling
- about 350g firm brined halloumi cheese (see page 23)
- 2 tbsp dried mint
- 1 large leek, washed, diced and cooked in a little olive oil until soft
- 2 tbsp Turkish red pepper paste (a very hot and spicy cooked-down pepper paste – optional)

1. Sift the flour, salt and dried yeast into a mixing bowl.

2. I like to use a digital scale here. Zero the scale with the bowl on it and measure the water and yoghurt on to the flour mixture.

3. Mix with a large spoon – it will feel very wet. Cover with a clean tea towel and leave to stand for 10 minutes.

4. After 10 minutes, give the dough another vigorous mix in the bowl. Oil your hands and also the work surface, then turn the dough out and give it a good knead for a couple of minutes.

5. Put the dough back into the bowl and leave for 1 hour.

6. When ready to cook the flatbreads, pull off balls of dough each weighing roughly 100g and roll out on a lightly floured surface. You want them to be cardboard thin, oval-shaped and roughly 23cm (like a small pizza) in length.

7. On to one half of each oval, grate about a tablespoon of halloumi. Add a teaspoon of dried mint and 2 teaspoons of the cooked leeks. If using, lightly smear blobs of the pepper paste on to the filling.

8. Fold the other half of the dough over the filling and pinch the seams of the gözleme shut. Roll very lightly to flatten and seal. (see photos on pp. 210–211)

9. Cook each gözleme in a dry frying pan over a moderate heat until the outside begins to blister and turn nut brown in some spots. Turn over and cook the other side.

10. When ready, turn out on to a chopping board, cut into strips and serve immediately.

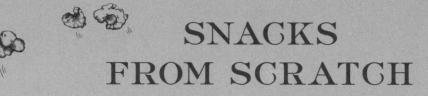

SNACKS
FROM SCRATCH

'Have we got any snacks?' is the collective cry just as the door slams shut. If you have young children, foolish is the attempt to leave home without a stash of snacks up your sleeve or in your handbag. In fact I'd go so far as to say it is an anthem of parenthood. And shops surely know it. Wily displays of eye-high snacks at the checkout are an all too obvious sales pitch to a hungry, tired, even bored child.

Children need refuelling often; it helps them grow, in fact. Three meals a day together with two or three healthy snacks is what's needed. That plaintive 'snack' wail has efficacy after all.

Crisps and biscuits are all well and good as an occasional treat on the hoof, and one my kids all enjoy. But for optimum snacking day in, day out, I'd far rather make my own. Cheaper and with the gratifying certainty of there being no nasties, I'm a past master at knocking together tempting and nutritional snacks to accompany adventures near and far.

Fruit leather, breadsticks, oat cakes and more have all passed muster with my daughter's keen-eyed and ever-hungry playdate friends. Replicating popular treats by making them yourself at home need not be onerous and is a crafty swipe at those in the 'kids' snacks' industry.

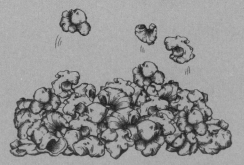

STRAWBERRY LEATHER

Rollable, windable and whipable – much like those shop-bought versions. You know the ones: DayGlo colours with a great big roaring bear on the front.

Use any soft seasonal fruit (strawberries, apricots, plums, blueberries, raspberries) and add cooking apples to the mix to help with the set and reduce the cost.

The preparation is simple, and although the cooking itself can take twelve hours in a low oven, cook it overnight and you won't notice the wait. Alternatively, you can use a dehydrator, which will cut the cooking time considerably.

Peel the sheet of dehydrated fruit from the paper and cut it into thin strips to roll up and wrap in squares of greaseproof for lunchboxes or snacks.

~ ~ ~ ~

Makes about 18 finger-width strips/rolls

- 300g Bramley apples (roughly 2 fist-sized apples), peeled, cored and cut into chunks
- 500g strawberries, hulled (or other soft seasonal fruit)
- cooking oil – a tiny trickle to oil the greaseproof paper

1. Preheat the oven to 50°C. If you have a gas oven, set it as low as it will go. Line a baking sheet with very lightly oiled greaseproof paper.
2. Put the fruit into a pan with a lid and cook, covered, over a medium heat until completely soft – about 10 minutes.
3. Push the pulp through a sieve into a bowl.
4. Pour on to the prepared baking sheet (the purée should be about 5mm thick in an even layer).
5. Put into the oven and leave overnight (or about 12 hours). It should feel leathery and dry to touch when done.
6. Peel off the paper and cut into whatever shapes you like. I prefer long strips to roll up. Store in an airtight container. Stored well, this will keep for at least a few weeks.

LEMONADE
SCONES

My husband is a New Zealander, and his is a family that loves to bake. One elderly aunt in particular bakes at quite a pace. For afternoon tea, she likes to make no less than eight different kinds of biscuits and cakes. Distracting though all that coconut frosting, chocolate twirls and fondant icing can be, it is her scones that really stand out.

Her secret? A small can of lemonade. I'd never heard of such a thing before. Just three main ingredients – minutes to make. The trick with scones is to bring the ingredients together swiftly and with as little mixing as possible. The sparkling drink seems to give the flour and cream a gravitational and fizzy hike. The scones are light in texture and have a terrific crust.

~ ~ ~ ~

Makes 8 scones
- 375g self-raising flour
- 170ml double cream
- 170ml lemonade (roughly half a can)

1. Preheat the oven to 220°C/gas mark 7.
2. Sift the flour into a bowl. Make a well in the middle and add the cream and lemonade. With a spoon, bring all the ingredients together quickly and with as little mixing as possible. The dough should be cohesive but airy and moist.
3. Turn out on to a lightly floured surface. You can either break the dough into 8 similar-size pieces and give each a quick shape with your hands, or gently roll it into a giant sausage shape and cut it into 8.
4. Lightly flour a baking tray and arrange the 8 pieces of dough side by side and slightly touching each other.
5. Bake in the oven until nicely browned and crisp on top – between 12 and 15 minutes.
6. Best eaten warm or on the day they are baked.

VARIATION: GINGER BEER SCONES

If wanting to make ginger beer scones, use 170ml of ginger beer instead of the lemonade and 2 tsp of ground ginger. These are especially nice served with soup – pumpkin, for example, at lunchtime.

SESAME BREADSTICKS

Breadsticks are a staple of the snack cupboard. Those aerated cardboard ones you can buy are just that – air. Making your own is a doddle. Simply bread dough knocked into strips and baked. Sesame is popular with my kids and a batch of these lasts no time at all.

~ ~ ~ ~

Makes about 15 breadsticks

- ½ recipe of basic bread dough (see page 30), made up to step 4 of the method
- 2 tsp sesame oil, plus extra for helping the sesame seeds to stick
- 3 tsp sesame seeds
- coarse polenta or olive oil, for the baking sheet (optional)

1. When the dough has doubled in size, take it out of the bowl and knock it back, mixing in the sesame oil as you do so.
2. Divide the dough into about 15 thin finger-width strips and roll out to about 15 cm – give each strip a twist or two along the length to stop the dough bulging too much in the oven.
3. Lightly sprinkle a baking sheet with polenta or, if you'd rather, lightly grease with olive oil, and position the breadsticks, spaced apart, on the prepared baking sheet.
4. With your finger, lightly trail each breadstick with some more sesame oil and sprinkle with the sesame seeds.
5. Let the breadsticks rest on the tray for 15 minutes before baking.
6. Meanwhile, preheat the oven to 180°C/gas mark 4. Bake the breadsticks for 15–20 minutes, until golden and crisp.
7. Remove from the baking sheet and cool on a wine rack.

POPCORN

Pop-pop-popcorn. At home we regularly make small amounts of popping corn. Cooked simply in a pan over a high heat with a spot of oil and served plain, popcorn is high in fibre, low in fat and contains no sugar or sodium. A million miles from the flabby, gargantuan tubs you get at the cinema.

As for microwaving popcorn, I just can't fathom why you would. With supervision, a glass-lidded saucepan is an exciting window through which children may watch those seemingly impenetrable kernels exploding into puffs of edible foam.

~ ~ ~ ~

Plain, basic popcorn

Makes enough to fill 2 sandwich bags
- 1 tbsp sunflower/vegetable oil – 50g popping corn

1. Use a heavy-based pan with a sturdy handle and a tight-fitting (glass!) lid.
2. Put the pan over a medium heat. Add the oil and corn. Lid it and heat, shaking occasionally, until the corn starts to pop. Turn up the heat and shake constantly. Hold your nerve and keep the pan lidded without peeking. You want the popcorn to pop as quickly as possible and a hot, steamy, lidded pan helps.
3. Once the frantic popping slows to 2–3 seconds between pops, remove from the heat and pour into a large bowl. Remove any unpopped or partially popped kernels you see.

~ ~ ~ ~

Smoked Paprika and Spice
- 1 tsp smoked paprika
- 1 tsp each cumin and fennel seeds, toasted and ground (see page 12)
- sea salt (optional)
- 1 tbsp olive oil or (or another oil if you prefer)

1. Mix together the ground spices (and the salt if using) in a small bowl.
2. Transfer your freshly popped hot popcorn to a larger container (one that has a lid), then add the spice mixture and drizzle the olive oil on top. Close the lid and shake until the popcorn is evenly coated with the spices.

~ ~ ~ ~

Salt and Sarson's
- Salt
- Malt vinegar (I use Sarson's)

1. Season the still hot and popped corn with salt and vinegar, as you like.

Buttered Maple and Spice

- 50g butter
- 2 tbsp maple syrup
- ½ tsp ground cinnamon
- ¼ tsp ground ginger
- a pinch of freshly grated nutmeg
- a pinch of sea salt (optional)

1. While the popcorn is popping, in a separate pan melt the butter over a medium heat until the sediment starts to turn golden brown.

2. Add the maple syrup and spices and swirl to mix. Tip the popped corn into this buttery mix with a pinch of salt (optional), lid the pan, and give it a good shake.

ELDERFLOWER SGROPPINO

Slushy ice, in other words. In Italy, sgroppino is a grown-up concoction of Prosecco, vodka and sorbet served as a cocktail. I make this elderflower version for my children on especially hot days. By all means make a Prosecco version when the kids have hit the sack.

~ ~ ~ ~

Serves 4

- 8 ice-cream scoops of lemon sorbet or elderflower sorbet (see page 237)
- about 200ml sparkling elderflower pressé, or elderflower cordial (see page 235) mixed with sparkling water
- fresh mint or lemon balm leaves, to serve

1. Place the sorbet scoops in a jug and add the sparkling elderflower pressé to the jug.

2. Whisk together by hand until combined and you have a thick slushy ice.

3. Divide the slushy sorbet between 4 glasses and stir each with a spoon, topping up with a little more elderflower pressé if needed.

4. Top each glass with a mint or lemon balm leaf to make it look especially lovely.

OAT CAKES

These oat biscuits have saved my bacon many times. Equally popular with a lump of cheese (perhaps a scraping of Marmite too?), or smeared with honey. Keep the raw roll of dough in the fridge for a few days and cut off the biscuits to cook fresh as and when required.

~ ~ ~ ~

Makes about 20 biscuits
- 150g rolled oats, plus a little extra for dusting
- a pinch of salt
- 100g wholemeal flour
- 35g soft light brown sugar
- 100g cold unsalted butter, diced
- 1 tsp baking power
- 60ml milk

1. Put the oats into a blender or food processor and blitz for 10 seconds or so, to grind them down to an oaty dust. Add the rest of the ingredients apart from the milk and process until the mixture resembles crumbs.

2. Tip the mix into a mixing bowl and add the milk. Combine to form a cohesive dough – but don't overwork it.

3. Dust a work surface with oats, then scrape out the dough and squash together gently into a large sausage shape (oat cake size in diameter). Make sure the sausage is evenly covered with the oats, then wrap in clingfilm and give it another roll to make sure the shape is nicely cylindrical. Refrigerate for 30 or so minutes, to firm up.

4. Meanwhile preheat the oven to 180°C/gas mark 4 and line a baking sheet with baking parchment.

5. Using a very sharp knife, slice the roll into 5–10mm – thick biscuits and carefully place on the prepared baking sheet. They are quite fragile but will harden when cooked.

6. Bake for 12–15 minutes, until crisp, going golden and also slightly brown around the edges.

7. Cool on a wire rack, though they are delicious still slightly warm too.

FRESH FRUIT

We've got the most enormous fruit bowl taking up half the table at home. It's so big, I bathed all my babies in it when the bathtub seemed to swamp them.

As the years have unfolded and my girls have grown too big for the fruit bowl, apples, pears, peaches and nectarines have been piled in and have looked almost as lovely as the babies. To fill and maintain the fruit bowl is quite a challenge. My children like to eat lots of fruit. In the blink of an eye, the bowl is empty and a few desultory grapes or an overly mottled banana are all that remains.

We have a tremendous greengrocer within walking distance from our house. Its double doors open on to the street, with fruit and vegetables in brightly coloured boxes hijacking pavement space. The stripy canopy at the front has been my pushchair respite from rain, sun and snow. It is also where I stand and take stock of what I might like to buy.

My use of fruit throughout the year is high. The obligatory piece of fruit in packed lunches and for playschool fruit bowls is one thing, as is the apple thrown into my handbag as a back-up snack (meant for me, more often than not eaten by one of my children). As such, a piece of fresh fruit, flawlessly ripe and resplendent in its season, is perfect just as it is. But a glut of fruit is another thing altogether.

On the drive to my mother's house, we pass through the orchards of Herefordshire. In the autumn hand-painted signs lie propped up on the roadside advertising apples, pears and plums. As car journeys with children go, it's quite a distraction to drive away with a box of plums, blue-black and dusted so. Even we, a family of fruit bats, can't eat a whole box of plums fast enough without them turning.

Cooking fresh fruit always feels decadent, almost as if you should be capable of consuming it with a greater gusto. That said, the synergy of sweet ripe blackberries with some sugar and more, in a cake or pie and introduced to the heat of an oven, makes for something so outrageous, so deliciously worthwhile you might as well go full circle and buy more fruit to fulfil this purpose.

CHERRY YOGHURT CAKE

A friend of a friend, Nina Kazanina, gave me this Russian cake recipe. It keeps well and is the happy recipient of any soft fruit, my favourites being cherries, hedgerow blackberries and raspberries. In winter, use those bags of frozen berries from the supermarket.

~ ~ ~ ~

Makes one 900g loaf or 20cm round cake

- semolina or plain flour, for dusting
- 2 eggs
- 180g caster sugar
- 200g plain yoghurt
- 200g plain flour
- 2 tsp baking powder
- a few drops of vanilla extract (optional)
- 300g stoned cherries/blackberries/ raspberries (any soft fruit – fresh or frozen)
- icing sugar, for dusting

1. Preheat the oven to 180°C/gas mark 4. Prepare a 900g loaf tin or 20cm round cake tin by lightly oiling or buttering the base and sides and sprinkling it with semolina or plain flour.
2. In a mixing bowl, whisk the eggs and sugar together.
3. Add the yoghurt, baking powder, flour and vanilla extract and mix well with a whisk to combine.
4. Pour half the mix into the prepared tin.
5. Spread the cherries or other soft fruit over in an even layer. Cover with the remaining batter mix.
6. Put into the oven and bake for 35–40 minutes. The top should be firm and beginning to turn golden brown in places.
7. Leave to cool in the tin for 10 minutes, then turn out on to a wire rack. Best dusted with icing sugar and eaten cold.

~ ~ ~ ~ ~ ~ ~ ~ ~ ~ ~ ~

BANANA BREAD

Makes one 900g loaf

- 75g unsalted butter melted, plus extra for greasing
- 3 or 4 ripe and very ripe bananas, peeled and mashed on a plate with a fork
- 1 medium egg, beaten
- 200g caster sugar (reduce to 150g if you like; it will do the cake no harm)
- 1 tsp vanilla extract
- 1 tsp bicarbonate of soda
- a pinch of salt
- 180g plain flour

1. Preheat the oven to 180°C/gas mark 4 and grease a 900g loaf tin with butter.
2. In a big bowl and with a wooden spoon, mix the melted butter, mashed banana, beaten egg, sugar and vanilla extract together.
3. Sprinkle the bicarbonate of soda and salt over the mixture and mix thoroughly. Then sift in the flour last and mix to combine.
4. Pour the mixture into the prepared loaf tin.
5. Bake for 1 hour – until a skewer comes clean from the centre.
6. Cool on a wire rack for 10 minutes before removing from the tin. Also great served toasted.

PEAR & BAY LEAF UPSIDE-DOWN CAKE

A bay leaves isn't just for stockpots and stews. Used in sweet cooking, its sweetly perfumed notes of allspice and clove really shine. With pear, it is an exceptional match. Never ever use the dried sort for, in my experience, there's always a bay tree or even a bay hedge nearby.

~ ~ ~ ~

MAKES ONE 24CM CAKE

- 80g unsalted butter, diced, plus a bit more for greasing
- 120g soft light brown sugar
- 300g (about 4) pears, peeled, cored and cut lengthways into 4 or 6 wedges/slices (size dependent)
- 4 bay leaves
- 150g caster sugar
- 175g plain flour
- 1 heaped tsp baking powder
- 2 tsp ground ginger
- a pinch of salt
- 150ml sunflower oil
- 2 large eggs, lightly beaten

1. Preheat the oven to 180°C/gas mark 4. Grease a 24cm round springform cake tin with a little butter and line it with a round piece of greaseproof paper, pressing it right into the corners and up the sides.

2. Scatter the brown sugar and butter over the bottom of the lined tin and put into the oven for 5 minutes, to melt together.

3. Remove from the oven and press three-quarters of the pear pieces and all the bay leaves (in an attractive pattern, if you like) into the melted butter and sugar in the tin.

4. Grate the remaining pear pieces, using a box grater.

5. Sift the caster sugar, flour, baking powder, ground ginger and salt in a large bowl, then beat in the oil and eggs and add the grated pear.

6. Spread the mix over the pears in the tin and return the cake tin to the oven for 40–45 minutes, or until a skewer comes out clean.

7. Allow the cake to cool a bit before folding back the edges of the greaseproof paper and releasing the sides of the tin. Turn the cake upside down on to a plate.

GRAPE FOCACCIA

Focaccia is an early form of pizza, a simple yeasted bread dough studded with flavour, smothered with olive oil and baked.

Where focaccia is different from a loaf of bread is in the process of flattening and flavouring the dough. With firm claw-like fingers, dimple the risen dough and deposit the grapes deep into the waiting pockets. Be sure not to go through the dough to the other side – just deep enough for them to remain embedded during the baking process.

Stoned cherries, stoned and chopped apricots, peaches, and even cubes of cooked pumpkin with fresh rosemary and rock salt, work well with this recipe.

~ ~ ~ ~

Makes one 44 x 30cm focaccia
- 6 tbsp olive oil, for oiling your hands and surface for the initial knead and for drenching the cooked focaccia
- 1 recipe of basic bread dough (see page 30), made up to step 4 of the method – do not knock it back
- 20 or so seedless black grapes

1. Preheat the oven to 220°C/gas mark 7.
2. Use 1 tablespoon of the oil to grease a 44 x 30cm baking tray, then tip the proven dough out on to the greased tray. With a rolling pin, roll once to the left and once to the right from the centre of your dough. You don't want to squash all the air out of the proven dough; you just want to shape it outwards and along the tin and for it to be approximately 2cm thick.
3. Cover with the tea towel and rest again for 40 minutes.
4. With firm claw-like fingers, press the surface of the dough down (taking care not to go through the dough to the bottom of the tin).
5. Push the grapes deep into the fingermark holes. With another tablespoon of olive oil rubbed into your hands, gently coat the entire surface of your loaf.
6. Bake in the oven for 10 minutes, then turn it down to 190°/gas mark 5 and bake for a further 20 minutes or so, until crusted and golden brown.
7. On exit from the oven, immediately pour the remaining olive oil over the focaccia – the hot dough will suck the oil up. This will give your focaccia its characteristic chewy crust.
8. Leave to cool slightly in the tin before cutting.

ORANGE, CRANBERRY & WALNUT SALAD

Hooray for oranges served savoury!

~ ~ ~ ~

Serves 4

- 4 ripe oranges, peeled
- 1 small red onion
- 2 tbsp red wine vinegar
- 75g dried cranberries
- 2 tbsp chopped toasted
  (see page 64) walnuts (optional)
- a handful of fresh flat-leaf
  parsley leaves, chopped
- 6 tbsp extra-virgin olive oil
- salt and freshly ground
  black pepper

1. Cut the oranges into thin slices and arrange on a serving platter.
2. Thinly slice the red onions and, in a small bowl, mix with the vinegar and leave to macerate for 5 minutes.
3. Drain the onions from the vinegar and scatter the onion slices over the orange slices.
4. Then add the cranberries, walnuts and parsley.
5. Mix the oniony vinegar with the olive oil, salt and freshly ground pepper to make a dressing. Spoon over the salad and serve.

CORDIALS

I love making cordials at home and find them far more delicious and economical than the shop-bought versions. The sugar in these recipes means they will keep very well in the fridge for a week or two before spoiling but are not so high in sugar as to keep unrefrigerated indefinitely.

For cordials to have any longevity, you'll need to be rigorous about sterilizing bottles, use higher levels of sugar and possibly even a preserving agent such as citric acid. Personally, I would rather make smaller quantities of different cordials, consuming them at their most fragrant in the first few days after they have been made.

I find the best dilution for these cordials with still or fizzy water to be 1:3. If you'd rather make sorbet with them, you'll need to dilute the solution much less, say half/half. The sugar content needs to be higher for the solution not to freeze too solid and to give these ices their scoopable quality.

Lemon cordial

Apart from scalding the lemon rind with the hot sugar syrup, get your children to make this lemonade from scratch – squashing, squeezing and mixing to taste.

~ ~ ~ ~

Makes about 300ml
- 150g caster sugar
- 300ml cold water
- 3 large lemons
  (preferably unwaxed)

1. Put the sugar and water into a pan and bring to the boil.
2. Peel, grate or zest the lemons into a bowl (avoiding the pith, as it is bitter).
3. Pour the just-boiled syrup over the zest. Leave to cool.
4. Add the juice of the lemons.
5. Strain and store in a sterilized (see page 175), sealed bottle in the fridge. This will keep perfectly well for up to 2 weeks, but the flavour is most fragrant if used within a couple of days.
6. Dilute as required with still or fizzy water to taste. We found 1:3 cordial to water to be best.

Note: To serve, you can add fresh mint leaves, strips of ginger, cucumber slices, lemon balm, elderflower or borage blossom. Not only do these look lovely, they also impart different flavours to the lemonade.

Elderflower cordial

In late spring, early summer, elder trees come into blossom. Picking the pale and frothy heads is a satisfying and scented task. Collect the blossom on a dry day and choose fragrant flowers that have only just begun to open, with some individual flowers still closed and absolutely none of them turning brown.

My preference for making small batches of different cordials goes awry when it comes to elderflower. So popular with my children, I almost can't pick enough of the blossom to make sufficient cordial to last the summer, let alone the year. I am greedy and attempt to pick masses of blossom in the short time it is at its best. To keep the cordial in tiptop condition, freeze it in small batches in small, used water bottles to defrost and dilute as needed.

~ ~ ~ ~

Makes 1.5 litres
- 25 generous heads of elderflower
- zest and juice of 2 lemons (preferably unwaxed)
- 1.5 litres boiling water
- 1kg caster sugar

1. Carefully pick over the elderflower heads, removing any insects. Put the flowers into a bowl with the lemon zest.
2. Pour the water into the bowl, making sure all the flowers get fully immersed in the water to prevent them oxidizing and turning brown.
3. Cover with a clean tea towel and leave overnight to infuse.
4. Strain the liquid through a clean jelly bag or piece of muslin into a large pan.
5. Add the sugar and the juice of the lemons.
6. Bring to the boil, skim off any froth that surfaces and simmer for 2 minutes, stirring well to ensure that all the sugar has dissolved.
7. Leave to cool, then pour what syrup you plan to use immediately into a sterilized container or bottle and store in the fridge. Pour the remaining cordial into clean plastic bottles and store in the freezer for up to a year.
8. Dilute as required with still or fizzy water to taste. We found 1:3 cordial to water to be best.

Rhubarb cordial

Not strictly a fruit, rhubarb makes a fantastically pretty pink drink.

~ ~ ~ ~

Makes about 500ml

- 500g trimmed rhubarb –
  the pinker the better
- 500ml cold water
- 200g caster sugar

1. Coarsely chop the rhubarb into 2.5cm batons.
2. Put the rhubarb, water and sugar into a saucepan and bring to the boil, skimming off any froth that might surface.
3. Simmer for 10 minutes, until the rhubarb is soft and broken down.
4. Strain through muslin or a very fine sieve into a bowl. Do not force the rhubarb through, as this can cause the cordial to go cloudy.
5. Dilute as required with still or fizzy water to taste. We found 1:3 cordial to water to be best.
6. Store in a sterilized bottle (see page 175) in the fridge for up to a week.

Note: Store the sieved rhubarb pulp in the fridge and stir through plain yoghurt or, even better, Bircher muesli (see page 73).

~ ~ ~ ~ ~ ~ ~ ~ ~ ~ ~ ~

CORDIAL SORBET

Serves 4

- 200g caster sugar
- peel and juice ½ a lemon
- 500ml cold water
- 250ml cordial (see above and
  page 234–5)

1. Place the sugar, lemon peel and water in a pan and bring to the boil, then stir until the sugar dissolves.
2. Take off the heat and allow to cool. Remove the lemon peel and stir in the cordial and the lemon juice.
3. Chill in the fridge for about 4 hours (or overnight).
4. Churn in an ice-cream maker according to the manufacturer's instructions, or pour into a freezer container and leave in the freezer, stirring every hour until frozen, for about 6 hours – this method will give you a slightly coarser, granita-style ice.
5. Remove from the freezer a few minutes before serving to allow it to soften.

PRESERVED FRUIT

Dried fruit, for me, is synonymous with childhood. Countless are the egg cups of raisins my granny used to offer me by way of a snack after school. My own children have gummed their way through bags and bags of dried apricots while teething. Mango, peach, pear, pineapple – all sticky and held tight in clenched little baby fists, sucked away but for a final pulpy lump caught somewhere underneath their chin.

When I started cooking professionally, and was stuck on the odd pastry shift (definitely the worst for me) with free rein to make puddings, the preservation of fresh fruit by means of drying, bottling and pickling was part of the prep list and began to fascinate me. In a busy restaurant kitchen an arsenal of dried fruit is a necessity. Puddings still need to be made on a Sunday when your last fresh fruit and veg delivery was Saturday morning – a busy two kitchen services now past and with all your prep wiped out. It is then that these sweetly shrivelled fruits, first plumped in liquid, then used on their own or baked alongside other ingredients, really come into their own. Prunes, apricots, figs, dates – the more the merrier.

There is a certain amount of exhilaration to be had in finishing a mammoth bottling session, charged as it always is with the anticipation of whether it will be enough to get me through to next year. It's a timely reminder of a summer spent when you can pop a jar of bottled apricots on the table to eat on top of a bowl of porridge in the middle of winter.

And perhaps most gratifying of all is the pickling of fruit for savoury use. Salted citrus fruits to use in tagines and dressings or to be chopped and mixed through grain salads offer a wonderful piquancy and depth of flavour. As for pickled rhubarb – not a fruit but near as dammit – it's the prettiest pickle of all. Serve as a condiment with crisp fried fillets of mackerel, herring or roast pork.

ECCLES CAKES

My favourite pastry. Hot or cold. On its own or served with some cheese. Lancashire or Cheddar would be my preference.

~ ~ ~ ~

Makes about 10 cakes

- 40g unsalted butter
- 90g soft light brown sugar
- 200g currants
- ½ tsp ground allspice
- ¼ tsp freshly grated nutmeg
- 300g all-butter shop-bought puff pastry (or make cheat's rough-puff pastry on page 166)
- plain flour, for dusting
- 2 egg whites, lightly beaten
- 2 tbsp caster sugar

1. In a small saucepan, melt the butter and brown sugar together, then add the currants and spices and mix well. Leave to cool.

2. Preheat the oven to 200°C/gas mark 6 and line a baking sheet with baking parchment.

3. Roll out the pastry on a floured worktop to 5mm thick, then use a glass or pastry cutter about 12cm wide to cut the pastry into rounds. Put a dessertspoonful of filling into the centre of each round, pull up the sides to cover the filling, then pinch the edges of the pastry together to enclose it.

4. Turn over the Eccles cake and place it, joined side down, on the prepared baking sheet. Repeat with the rest of the pastry and filling, then brush the cakes with beaten egg white.

5. Slash the surface of each cake three times with a sharp knife, then dust with the caster sugar.

6. Bake for 15–20 minutes, until well browned and crispy.

7. Serve hot or cold.

MALT LOAF

Tea-soaked dates and dark treacly muscovado sugar. The best thing about malt loaf is that it gets stickier and tastier the longer you leave it.

~ ~ ~ ~

Makes two 450g loaves
- vegetable oil for greasing
- 175g malt extract
- 85g dark muscovado sugar
- 300g pitted dates
- 150ml hot black tea
- 2 large eggs, beaten
- 250g plain flour
- 1 tsp baking powder
- ½ tsp bicarbonate of soda

1. Preheat the oven to 150°C/gas mark 2. Grease two 450g loaf tins and line with strips of baking parchment.
2. Put the malt extract, sugar and dates into a mixing bowl and pour over the hot tea. Allow the dates to soften for 5 minutes, then purée in a blender or food processor. Put them back into the bowl, add the eggs and stir well.
3. Sift in the flour, baking powder and bicarbonate of soda, quickly stir and pour into the prepared tins. Bake for 50 minutes until firm, well risen and a skewer insert in the middle comes out clean.
4. Allow to cool a little, then remove from the tins.
5. Serve sliced and buttered.

~ ~ ~ ~ ~ ~ ~ ~ ~ ~ ~ ~

DRIED APRICOTS WITH CARDAMOM SYRUP

A terrific thing to have in the fridge – serve with Greek yoghurt, thick cream or ice cream as a pudding, with porridge for breakfast, or use for baking in tarts and pastries.

~ ~ ~ ~

Makes 2 jars
- 500ml cold water
- 75g caster sugar
- juice of ½ a lemon
- 10 green cardamom pods, crushed
- 1 vanilla pod, split in half lengthwise
- 250g dried apricots

1. In a non-reactive pan, combine the water, sugar, lemon juice, cardamom and vanilla pod. Bring to the boil, then simmer for 5 minutes.
2. Reduce the heat to its lowest, then add the apricots and very gently simmer without boiling for 2 minutes.
3. Remove from the heat and leave the apricots to plump up in the syrup for about 5 hours.
4. Transfer to sterilized dry jars (see page 58) and refrigerate. If you can, leave the apricots for a couple of days before serving.

EARL GREY & ORANGE PRUNES

Prunes made more marvellous. The longer you can leave them before opening the jar, the better – the syrup takes on the prune flavour and the prunes take on the tea flavour. Serve with Greek yoghurt as a pudding or with porridge in the morning.

~ ~ ~ ~

Makes two 450ml jars
- 40g soft light brown sugar
- 400ml hot weak Earl Grey tea
- 250g Agen or other large good-quality pitted prunes
- 150ml orange juice (you could use brandy or armagnac instead)
- 2 fresh bay leaves
- zest of 1 orange
- 1 cinnamon stick
- 1 vanilla pod

1. You will need two 450g airtight jars, sterilized (see page 58).
2. Dissolve the sugar in the hot tea and leave to cool. Pour the tea over the prunes in a lidded tub and put them aside to soak overnight. It is not necessary to refrigerate them.
3. Strain the liquid into a pan and add the orange juice and the rest of the ingredients. Bring to the boil, then turn down the heat and simmer for 5 minutes.
4. Divide the prunes between the two jars and pour the syrup over them, making sure the prunes are immersed. Seal the jars with a lid and store in the fridge.
5. These prunes improve the longer you leave them and will keep well, sealed and refrigerated, for up to 3 months.

~ ~ ~ ~ ~ ~ ~ ~ ~ ~ ~

PICKLED RHUBARB

Makes about 2 jars
- 200ml cider or white wine vinegar
- 250g caster sugar
- 1 cinnamon stick
- a pinch of chilli flakes
- 1 globe of crystallized ginger in syrup, cut into shreds (optional)
- 1 red onion, finely diced
- 350g trimmed rhubarb, cut into 4cm lengths

1. Put the vinegar and sugar into a pan and bring to the boil, while the sugar dissolves. Add the cinnamon stick, chilli flakes and ginger and simmer for 5 minutes.
2. Add the onions and simmer gently, uncovered, for 10 more minutes. The onions will become soft and the mixture thicker.
3. Now add the rhubarb and simmer gently for about 4 more minutes, or until the rhubarb is just tender. Don't overcook – you want the fruit to remain pink and the pieces intact; you are not making a chutney.
4. Leave to cool. Stored in the fridge in a tub, bowl or a couple of jars, this will keep for weeks.

PRUNE & APPLE CROUSTADE

The combination of baked prune and apple here is stupendous. And while a croustade might sound a little on the fancy side, in essence it is simply fruit baked in filo pastry. It can be helpful to make this with a 25cm ring mould or the outside of a springform cake tin, to help hold the croustade shape while you assemble it – but it isn't essential. Any cinnamon sugar you have left over can be stored in a jar and used as you might sugar (on porridge is a favourite).

~ ~ ~ ~

Makes one 25cm croustade

- 5 tbsp butter
- 4 Bramley apples, peeled, cored and cut into cubes
- 8–10 marinated prunes (see opposite page), drained of their soaking liquid and roughly chopped (keep the liquid to use when cooking the apples)
- 5 tbsp caster sugar, mixed with ½ tsp ground cinnamon
- 4 sheets of filo pastry (or 6 if they are small)

1. To make the filling, melt 1 tablespoon of the butter in a saucepan over a moderate heat. Add the apples and 2–3 tablespoons of the cinnamon sugar. Cook until just softened, about 5 minutes, then pour on about 2 tablespoons of the reserved prune liquid and cook until the liquid has disappeared. Remove from the heat and stir in the chopped prunes.

2. Preheat the oven to 190°C/gas mark 5. Line a baking tray with baking parchment and add the ring mould, if using.

3. Filo pastry dries out very quickly. Take out what you need for the recipe, then seal up the rest and return to the fridge. Keep a damp cloth over the filo you are working with.

4. Melt the remaining butter in a small pan and brush a little of the melted butter over the lined baking sheet.

5. Work with one filo sheet at a time. Lay a sheet of filo on a clean work surface and brush with melted butter, then sprinkle with a little of the remaining cinnamon sugar.

6. Lay the filo on the prepared baking sheet, overlapping the ring mould if using. Lay another sheet on top at right angles (to form a thick cross) and then repeat with the other two sheets.

7. Spoon the filling into the centre of the filo and fold the pastry edges over to enclose it. It should look crumpled and very rustic. If you have a gap when pulling the filo sheets together, simple cover with an extra sheet of filo brushed with butter.

8. Brush the whole croustade with any remaining melted butter and scatter over the remainder of the cinnamon sugar.

9. Remove the ring mould (if using), leaving the formed croustade on the baking sheet. Bake until the pastry is fully cooked and golden – this should take about 40 minutes.

10. Remove from the oven, slide on to a wire rack and leave to cool slightly.

11. Serve warm with ice-cream, crème fraîche or cream on the side.

SNAIL BREAD

A loose interpretation of a Chelsea, a copycat attempt at a breakfast cinnamon roll, and indulgence of a four-year-old's fondness for raisins. So-called snail bread, these whirly cinnamon buns are ace.

~ ~ ~ ~

Makes 12

- vegetable oil, for greasing
- 1 recipe of basic bread dough (see page 30), made up to step 5 of the method
- 75g unsalted butter, softened
- 75g light muscovado sugar
- 1 heaped dsp ground cinnamon
- 100g raisins
- sugar syrup to brush over the cooked snail bread (50g sugar/50g of water brought to the boil in a small pan and left to cool)

1. Roll out the dough on a lightly oiled work surface to an oblong (A3 size and 1cm thick).
2. Put the butter, sugar and cinnamon into a pan over a gentle heat and stir together until melted. Spoon the buttery mix all over the rolled-out dough.
3. Distribute the raisins evenly over the buttery dough.
4. Roll the dough – landscape view – up into a long worm. With a sharp knife cut the dough 'sausage' into 12 thick slices.
5. Place the whirly slices of dough, cut side up, touching and side by side, in rows of 3 or 4 on a greased and lined baking tray.
6. Lightly cover with a clean damp tea-towel and leave to prove for 30–45 minutes.
7. Meanwhile preheat the oven to 200°C/gas mark 6.
8. Put the tray of buns into the oven and cook for 10 minutes, then turn down the heat to 180°C/gas mark 4 and cook for a further 25 minutes.
9. Remove from the oven and brush the buns with the sugar syrup while still hot. Leave to cool on the tray. Best eaten on the day.

ORANGES & LEMONS
(SAY THE BELLS OF ST CLEMENT'S)

The salted and preserved sort.

~ ~ ~ ~

Makes one 500ml jar

- 6–8 lemons or oranges (use unwaxed ones, as you'll be eating the skins, or give waxed citrus fruit a good scrub with plenty of water and clean wire wool)
- about 1 tbsp coarse sea salt per lemon or orange
- lemon or orange juice, as needed

1. You will need a 500ml jar – a Kilner jar is perfect. Sterilize the jar in the oven for 10 minutes at 180°C/gas mark 4.

2. Scrub the lemons or oranges with a vegetable brush and dry them.

3. Remove the stalk of each fruit, then from the other end cut lengthwise downwards, stopping about 2cm from the base. Now make another downward slice, so you've cut an X into the fruit.

4. Spoon about 1 tablespoon of coarse salt into the lemon or orange where you made the cut and put the salt-filled lemons or oranges into the jar.

5. Press the lemons or oranges down firmly in the jar to extract some of the juice. Put on the lid and leave for a few hours or overnight.

6. When this time has passed, press the fruits down again to extract more juice as they start to soften. If they aren't submerged at this point, add more lemon or orange juice to cover.

7. Leave them somewhere cool and dark for at least 4 weeks, topping up the juice if the fruits become exposed. Once soft, they are ready to use. Store in the fridge, sealed in the jar for upwards of a year.

8. To use, remove as many lemons or oranges from the liquid as you need, rinse them and pat dry. Split the lemons or oranges in half and scrape out and discard the pulp. Slice the lemon or orange peel into thin strips or cut into small dice.

Note: Best used in slow-cooked dishes, salads or dressings to give a salty citrus tang.

CANDIED & CRYSTALLIZED ORANGE PEEL

This recipe is a great way to use up the orange skins from just-juiced oranges. More than just a baking ingredient, candied peel is a real treat. It takes a day or two for the peel to dry, so plan ahead. (Chocolate-dipped it's even better.)

~ ~ ~ ~

Makes 2 oranges' worth

- 2 large oranges
- 375g caster sugar

1. If using oranges from juicing, cut each half into 6 vertical segments. Alternatively, cut the whole orange into 6 and remove the flesh, scraping as much of the pith away as you can with a potato peeler and leaving 6 segments of orange peel.

2. Cook the segments in a large pan of boiling water for 15 minutes. Drain the peel and cook again in fresh boiling water for another 15 minutes, then drain again.

3. In a separate pan, bring 300g of the sugar and 300ml of water to the boil. Turn the heat down to medium and stir to dissolve the sugar.

4. Add the peel to the syrup and return to the boil, then reduce the heat and simmer until the peel is soft and translucent. This should take 45 minutes to 1 hour.

5. Drain and allow the candied peel to cool. You can keep the orange-flavoured syrup for cake baking or to spoon over plain yoghurt.

6. When cool, cut the peel to the size you like and either toss it in the remaining 75g of sugar inside a clean plastic bag, or press the segments into the sugar on a plate. Lift the peel from the sugar and lay out on greaseproof paper until the coating is completely dry. This should take 1–2 days.

VARIATION: CHOCOLATE-DIPPED CANDIED PEEL

If you do want to cover the peel in chocolate, simply melt 100g good-quality dark chocolate, then cut the peel to your chosen size and dip it in the chocolate. Leave to dry on greaseproof paper.

INDEX

With thanks to Matthew (you are amazing), my editor Sarah Lavelle, photographer Mike Lusmore, Isabel Davies and Alexei Janssen and also my godson Johann, St Matthew's Playgroup, Colston's Primary School, Laura Hart of Hart's Bakery, Tom Calver at Westcombe Dairy, James Brown of Fish and Trips of St Mawes, Ellen Hughes and Vic Stevens at Bristol Kitchen Radio, my greengrocer Gardener's Patch, Murray's the Butchers, Alex Lucas for the drawings, Barny Haughton, Kate Hawkings and Mark Taylor and lastly, of course, both my parents and their partners.

And extra-special thanks to my daughter's friends Alfie and Edie Blackmore, Hector, Bronte and Juno Carmichael-Sturrock and Erin, Angus, Inez and Sylvie White.